THOMAS FRANKLIN BURTON
THIRD SERGEANT, COMPANY A
13TH TENNESSEE CAVALRY U.S.
(BRADFORD'S BATTALION)

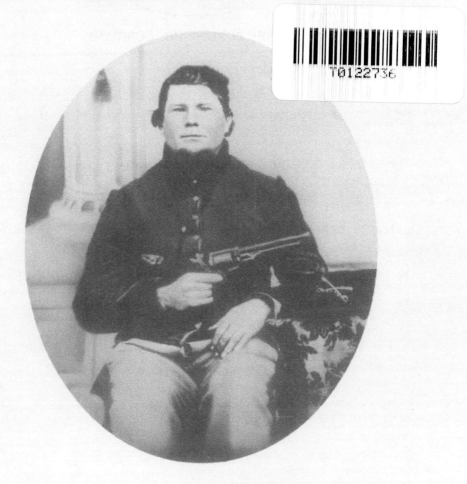

By
Keith C. Black

TURNER PUBLISHING COMPANY

TURNER PUBLISHING COMPANY

Project Coordinator: Herbert C. Banks II
Designer: David Hurst

Copyright ©1999 Keith Black
All rights reserved.
Publishing Rights: Turner Publishing Company.

This book or any part thereof may not be reproduced in any form without the express written consent of the author and publisher.

This publication was produced using available and submitted materials. The author and publisher regret they cannot assume liability for errors or omissions.

Library of Congress Catalog No. 99-61896
ISBN: 978-1-56311-510-3

LIMITED EDITION.

CONTENTS

"But none have borne themselves with more determined spirit of courage and bravery, a truer and more patriotic devotion to their country, or, in short, have won more brilliant record than our battalion at Fort Pillow"

Mack J. Leaming,
Lieut. and Adjutant 13th Reg't Tenn. Cavalry

ACKNOWLEDGMENTS

I would like to thank my friends, David, Leslie, Ken, Kevin, and Andy. Had it not been for our trip to Shiloh, I would not have tried to locate Thomas Burton.

I cannot thank my wife Debbie enough for her patience, interest and desire for her part in locating information on Thomas and Maranda.

I would also like to thank the following family members and relatives of Thomas Burton for their contribution to the information gathered within:

Glynda Black - Provided information and the charcoal picture of
        Thomas and Maranda

Oleta Swift - Provided family photographs and information on Thomas and
        Maranda

John Burton - Provided information on Thomas and Maranda

Gene Edwards - Provided information on Thomas and Maranda

Nancy Solfisburg - Provided family photographs and information

Clifton Ray - Provided information and tin type photograph of Thomas

Fort Pillow Park Ranger Nathan Moran Provided me with the casualty list from Fort Pillow, his kindness and personal interest in the Fort Pillow Battle was appreciated.

I would also like to extend My thanks to Private Carrol Sweeny's Descendant John T. Suttles for providing me with the picture and information on Mr. Sweeny. It was a privilage to meet a direct descendant of another soilder who had fought alongside Thomas at Fort Pillow.

Additional thanks go out to Nancy Solfisburg for her part in distributing hese books.

Special thanks to my wife's brother, Eddie Rhodes and his wife, Kay. Without their financial backing, this book could not have been published.

PREFACE

The purpose of gathering information contained within this book, is to allow the descendants of Thomas F. Burton to understand with as much detail that is available, about events that directly effected him and his family during the civil war.

The initial information gathered on Thomas was located by computer at the Shiloh National Military Park visitor center, this information listed Union and Confederate dead that were buried in military cemeteries at various locations in the United States. The information gathered on Thomas consisted of the Cavalry name, the Company Thomas was in, his rank, the place were he was captured, the prison he was taken too, the place were he died, the cause of death, and the location and stone number of his grave.

This information, and the knowledge that Thomas had fought and was captured during a failed attempt to hold Fort Pillow from Confederate General Nathan Bedford Forrest was interesting enough to keep me looking for more details into his participation and death during the Civil War.

Gathering information at Shiloh, Columbus Belmont, Fort Pillow, Andersonville Prison, Andersonville National Cemetery, Chickamauga, Tennessee State and Federal Archives, Murray State's Pogue Library, and finally multiple visits with Thomas's grandson, John Thomas Burton, his wife Ivanell, and his daughter Gene Burton Edward's compelled me to put this information in book form.

Since no documented information was made or could be found, personal information gathered within this book came from stories passed down by the descendants of Thomas and Maranda, the majority of information came from The Official Records Of The Civil War, State and Federal records, and other books as noted in the bibliography relating to locations and activities which occurred before, during, and or after Thomas's presence there.

During my search for information on Thomas, and the Civil War, I found that to this day there still exist emotional scars from descendants of both sides as a result of how the war was fought and its final outcome.

As many border state families have, I have relatives that fought for both the Union and for the Confederacy, and I am proud of each individuals contribution to the war, Union or Confederate they fought for their beliefs on how they thought this country should be governed.

I did not put this information together to place blame on the Union or Confederate Army, or any one person for actions that took place at Fort Pillow, Andersonville Prison, or any other locations mentioned, my only interest is to create a picture of what Thomas must have experienced while he was present at these locations.

This book is not professionally written, and I apologize for my lack of knowledge to do the same. I hope this book will help preserve Thomas' memory to all his present and future descendants and, in some way, help them have a clearer understanding about his participation and sacrifice for what he believed in during this turbulent period in our country's history.

John Burton (Thomas Franklin Burton's father) was born in Virginia in 1802, he and his wife Sara moved to New Providence some time in 1839. Thomas Allbritten (Maranda Allbritten's father) was born in Georgia in 1804, He and his wife Tabitha would have had to moved to New Providence prior to their 1st child Issac's birth which the 1850 Census shows him to be born in Kentucky on December 4th, 1830.

CALLOWAY COUNTY 1840 CENSUS & OTHER PERSONAL ACCOUNTS

Name	Males in Family	Females in Family	Total
1. John H. Burton	7	4	11
1. Thomas Allbritten	4	2	6

Notice that there were seven Burton males in the 1840 census and only 5 in the 1850 census that would have been old enough to be in the 1840 census. They may have lost 2 sons due to disease or injury or maybe other male members of their families lived with them during this time, and either died or moved out before the 1850 census was taken.

CALLOWAY COUNTY 1850 CENSUS & OTHER PERSONAL ACCOUNTS

Thomas Franklin Burton was the son of John H. and Sara R. Burton, Thomas was born in Virginia in 1830.

The family names and ages as of the 1850 Calloway County Census are as follows:

Name	Age	Occupation	Sex	State born	Died
1. John H. Burton	48 Born 1802	Farmer	M	VA	1860's
2. Sara R. Burton	40 Born 1810		F	NC	
3. Thomas F. Burton	20 Born 1830		M	VA	7/14/1864
4. Elizabeth	18 Born 1/12/1832		F	NC	1/14/1901
5.Martha	17		F	VA	
6. John J.	16		M	VA	
7. Robert A.	14 Born 1836		M	VA	1922
8. Charles S.	13 Born 1837		M	VA	
9. Mary H.	12 Born 1838		F	VA	
10. David M.	8 Born 1842		M	KY	10/11/1864
11. Virgina A.	1 Born 1849		F	KY	

Maranda Allbritten was the daughter of Thomas B. and Tabitha Allbritten, she was born in Calloway County Kentucky on the 12th day of June, 1832.

Maranda had four brothers and one sister,their names and ages as of 1850 are as follows:

Name	Age	Occupation	Sex	State Born	Land Value Pers Prop	Died
1. Thomas B. Allbritten	46 Born 1804	Farmer	M	GA		1861
2. Tabitha Allbritten	45 Born 1805		F	NC		
3. Isaac	19 Born 12/04/1830		M	KY		7/05/1912
4. Maranda	16 Born.6/12/1832		F	KY		12/15/1887
5. Thomas	12 Born 1838		M	KY		
6. William	11 Born 4/23/1838		M	KY		12/11/1887
5. James K. Polk	8 Born 10/?/1841		M	KY		1/10/1885
6. Mary (Aunt Sis)	6 Born 1844		F	KY		1930
7. Mary D. Steeley	46 Born 1804		F	NC		

Mary D. Steely may have been Tabitha's sister.

The Burton's and Allbritten's were farming property located in New Providence on the Kentucky and Tennessee state line before, during, and after the Civil War. They were thought to have grown corn, tobacco, and wheat.++

++ Information from John Thomas Burton - Grandson

CALLOWAY COUNTY 1860 CENSUS & OTHER PERSONAL ACCOUNTS

Notice that for some reason some of the ages have changed from previous census, Thomas Allbritten was shown to be one year older than Tabitha in the 1850 Census, but is now shown to be four years older in the 1860 Census. Also the name Mary D. Steely in the 1850 Census and Polly Steely in the 1860 Census may be the same person even though the ages are different, or it may be another one of Tabitha's family living with them after Mary Steely moved out or passed away before the 1860 Census.

It is interesting to note that the families land and personal property value are also listed in this Census.

Name	Age	Occupation	Sex	State Born	Land Value Pers Prop	Died
1.John H. Burton	57	Farmer	M	VA	$3,000 / $800	
2.Sara	50	Housewife	F	NC		
3.Martha	24		F	VA		
4.Mary	20		F	VA		
5.David	17		M	KY		10/11/186
6.Virginia	12		F	KY		
7.Missouri F.	8		F?	KY		

Name	Age	Occupation	Sex	State Born	Land Value Pers Prop	Died
1.Thomas Allbritten	57	Farmer	M	GA	$2,700 / $640	1861
2.Tabitha Allbritten	53	Housewife	F	NC		
3.William	21		M	KY		12/11/1887
4.James K. Polk	18		M	KY		1/10/1885
5.Mary (Aunt Sis)	16		F	KY		1930
6.Polly Steely	60		F	NC		

NOTE: Maranda's Parents, Brothers, Sisters, Polly Steely may be Tabitha's Sister.

Name	Age	Occupation	Sex	State Born	Land Value Pers Prop	Died
1.Isaac C. Allbritten	30	Farmer	M	KY ? ?		7/05/1912
2.Sarah P. Allbritten	26	Housewife	F	TN		
3.Mary M.	5		F	KY		
4.Tabias	4		M	KY		
5.Sandy	1		M	KY		

NOTE: Maranda's Brother Isaac's Family

Name	Age	Occupation	Sex	State Born	Land Value Pers Prop	Died
1.Thomas Allbritten	24	Farmer	M	KY	0 / $1,500	
2.Sarah F. Allbritten	24	Housewife	F	KY		
3.Martha	5		F	KY		
4.Sarah E.	3		F	KY		
5.Elizabeth J.	1		F	KY		

NOTE: Maranda's Brother Thomas's Family
For some unknown reason Thomas and Maranda were not listed in the 1860 Census.

Name	Age	Occupation	Sex	State Born	Land Value Pers Prop	Died
1.Robert Burton	24	Farmer	M	VA	$700 / $230	1922
2.Martha Burton	22	Housewife	F	GA		
3.Sara Hart	39		F	VA		
4.Winifred A. Hart	20		F	KY		
5.R.S. Hart	18		M	KY		

NOTE: Thomas's Brother Robert's Family

CALLOWAY COUNTY 1860 CENSUS & OTHER PERSONAL ACCOUNTS

Name	Age	Occupation	Sex	State Born	Land Value Pers Prop	Died
1.William R. Allbritten	35	Farmer	M	KY ?		12/5/1890
2.Elizabeth B. Allbritten	28	Housewife	F	VA		1/14/1901
3.James C.	13		M	KY		
4.Mary Jane	12		F	KY		
5.Francis	10		F	KY		
6.W.P.	7		M	KY		
7.Julia Ann	3		F	KY		
8.Charles Burton	23	Farmer	M	VA		

NOTE: Thomas's sister Elizabeth and her family and his Brother Charles Burton who lived with Elizabeth and William.

W.P. and Julia Ann are probably Elizabeth and William's children, the older children were from William's first marriage. William Redwine was hung by Guerrillas during the last years of the war, he survived.

Name	Age	Occupation	Sex	State Born	Land Value/Pers Prop	Died
1.Thomas Stubblefield	48	Farmer	M	N. Carolina ?		
2.Harriet	30	Housewife	F	Tennessee		
3.John C. Simmons	22		M	Tennessee		2/15/1900

John Simmons may have been Harriet Stubblefield's brother.

Above two photos: Thomas and Tabitha Allbritten's home in New Providence. Thomas Burton and Maranda Allbritten where married inside the house of the upper photograph on December 24th 1855 by C.M. Gatily in the presence of E. Henry and R. Allbritten.
Inset: Maranda Allbritten.

CIVIL WAR EVENTS BEFORE, DURING, AND AFTER THOMAS JOINED THE UNION ARMY

Thomas and the other men had not chosen sides until August of 1864, a little over three years after the War had begun.

The following events had already taken place before they had entered the Union Army:

The Confederates had fired on Fort Sumter on April 12th, 1861 to start the Civil War, The first battle of bull run was fought in July 1861, Grant arrived in Paducah Kentucky in September 1861, the battle at Fort Henry was fought in January 1862, Fort Donelson was captured by Grant in February 1862, the Battle for Shiloh was fought in April 1862,the Seven days Campaign was fought in June 1862, Memphis had surrendered in June of 1862, Second Battle for Bull Run was fought in August 1862, the Battle for Antietam was fought in September 1862, the Battle at Fredericksburg was fought in December 1862, Lincoln signs the Emancipation Proclamation in January 1863, Battle of Chancollorsville which claimed the life of Confederate General Stonewall Jackson was fought in May 1863, Siege of Vicksburg Begins in May 1863 and Ends July 4th 1863, the battle at Gettysburg was fought in July 1863.

The following events had taken place while Thomas had joined the Union Army, and was at Fort Anderson in Paducah.

The battles for Chickamauga was fought in September 1864, the Battle for Chattanooga was fought in November 1863, Lincoln delivers the Gettisburg address in November 1863.

The following battles had taken place while Thomas was at Fort Pillow.

Nathan Forrest's attempt to capture Paducah fails, and Confederate Colonel Duckworth captures Union City in March 1864.

The following battles had taken place after Thomas had been captured and confined in Andersonville Prison.

Battle of the Wilderness was fought May 1864, Cold Harbor & the battle for Kennesaw Mountain June 1864. Nathan Forrest's Battle at Brice's Cross Roads was fought in June 1864.

The following battles had taken place after Thomas had died in Andersonville, his younger brother David was still alive to have heard news of the following battles.

Atlanta surrendered in September. And the battle for Mobile Bay was fought in August 1864.

The following battles and the surrender of the Confederacy was completed after David Burton had died in October at Andersonville Prison.

The battle for Franklin was underway in November of 1864, Battle for Nashville was fought in December 1864, General Lee surrendered on April 9th, 1865, Nathan Forrest surrendered in May of 1865, Abraham Lincoln was assassinated by John Wilkes Booth.

WESTERN THEATER AND CALLOWAY COUNTY

The majority of people from Calloway County during the Civil War sympathized with the South. As the county did not lie along the immediate track of either army, and was altogether unimportant from a strategic point of view, it was not made the theater of any important military operation during the war. Only a few slight skirmishes occurred on its soil, and these were between small parties of the opposing forces, that from time to time passed through various parts of the county.#

During 1861 and 8162, before any Union occupation had begun, the people of New Providence were first exposed to the Confederate Army while they were constructing and defending Forts Heiman in Calloway County and Fort Henry directly across the river from Fort Heiman. It was during the construction of these forts that Confederate forces began impressment of Kentucky Whites for military duty and of Blacks and Unionist men for work on the twin river forts. The Burton's and Allbritten farms were a few miles East of Fort Heiman and located on the State Line Road which was used by both armies during the war. I suspect that the Confederate activities during the beginning of the war did have a negative effect on the people in the New Providence area, due to the fact that at least five men from that small region, all of which were related or knew each other, joined the Union Army to fight against the Confederates while living in a southern sympathizing County.

In January and February of 1862 the battles for Fort Henry and Fort Donelson were fought, the citizens of Calloway County and other surrounding counties were well aware of the battles being fought at both locations, These battles were close enough to New Providence that cannon fire from the Union Gunboats and both Confederate earthworks could be heard during the battles there.

The Federal victories at Fort Henry and Fort Donelson ensured that both Kentucky and Western Tennessee remained within the Union, however, a strong force of Confederate cavalry under Nathan Bedford Forrest remained in these areas to the dismay of both Grant and Sherman throughout the war.

In the latter part of 1863 a small detachment of Federals, numbering about 300, took possession of Murray, and threw up earthworks near the town, which they occupied for a short period of time. This was the only force of regular troops stationed in the town during the war.

The running of supplies to rebel soldiers across the Tennessee River at a landing known in recent years as Newburg, subsequently submerged in the creation of Kentucky Lake, was a source of constant irritation to the Union forces. Consequently, gunboats operating under the command of Gen. U.S. Grant would shell the place periodically to the extent it became known as Warburg during the conflict, later changed to Blood and eventually Newburg.

Out of necessity, armies were compelled to live off the land during occupation operations in the Civil War. As a result both sides of the struggle vied with each other in commandeering of horses, livestock and foodstuffs for both animals and men. Those efforts are not to be confused with guerrillas-the wolves of war. In many instances, perhaps in the majority, guerrilla bands were groups of deserting soldiers preying on the countryside in search of money and food, often wearing the tattered uniforms of the gray and of the blue.#

 # The Story Of Calloway County 1822 - 1976 - Jennings

The impact on the non-participating people by guerrillas was far greater than can be grasped by the present generation, guerrilla activities among the residents of the county reached staggering proportions with various estimates of 20 to 40 citizens being shot down in cold blood. Foodstuffs were buried in mounds over the farm in the winter months, cattle would be staked out in hollows and fence rows at night, the hours when marauders scourged the countryside. Women folks would bar doors and windows against feared attacks while fathers and sons who were left behind would stalk the shadows of homes and barns at night as protective sentinals.# At night Maranda Burton and her sister Mary (Aunt sis,McCuiston) would cover up the windows with quilts, and put a lamp in the fire place for light, this was done to convince the guerrillas that the house was vacated and not worthy of their attention.^^

Arson, rape, thieving and murder were commonplace, but must be admitted were the facts of war when mankind engages in mortal civil conflict. Our Civil War was no exception to the rule.

As for the men from Calloway County who enlisted into service during the Civil War, all recorded facts indicate the estimate of 800 men enlisting in the C.S.A. and 200 in the U.S.A. as being correct. With 1800 men within the county being recorded as of military age during the War Between the States, the comparison reflects a monstrous proportion of menfolks being actively engaged in the conflict.

while a majority of Calloway County men fought for the south, friends of the Union also rushed to arms. T.P. Carter recruited a Company of Cavalry in the County for the First Kentucky Battalion U.S.A., while a large number enlisted in the Fifteenth Kentucky Cavalry, and other Regiments.#

Union Army, Major William Bradford's Thirteenth Tennessee Cavalry

Company A, recruited a portion of Calloway County Men, 3rd Sergeant Thomas F. Burton, Corporal William R. Allbritten, Private William H. Allbritten, and Private John C. Simmons enlisted at Fort Anderson in Paducah Kentucky on August 18th 1863, Thomas's brother Corporal David M.Burton enlisted at Fort Anderson August 26th. The men were mustered into the U.S. Army on October 21st 1863. They where then mustered into the 13th Tennessee Cavalry Company A on December 5th 1863. The 13th Tn Cavalry scouted the surrounding country side until February 1864 when they were order by Chief Cavalry Officer William Sooey Smith to occupy **Fort Pillow** Tennessee. They were attacked by Confederate General Nathan Bedford Forrest and Virtually Anihilated.*

Fully 200 men from Calloway County fought under the stars and stripes and did valiant service defending the cause of the National Union.

Several Confederate Companies were recruited in Calloway County, the first of which was raised early in 1861, By Capt. C.C. Bowman.. This Company served one year in Virginia under Gen. Dick Taylor, but participated in no engagements of any note.#

The Confederate third Kentucky Infantry Company H was organized shortly after the breaking out of the war, and left for the front in April 1861. The Company numbered 87 men, only about 25 whom returned at the close of the war, the rest having fallen at Shiloh, Baton Rouge, Vicksburg, Oxford, **Fort Pillow**, Selma, Macon,

The Story Of Calloway County 1822 - 1976 - Jennings
^^Information provided by Oleta Swift - Great Granddaughter
* Information gathered at the Nashville Archives

Tishimingo Creek and other bloody battles in which the celebrated Kentucky Confederate Brigade participated, this same Company was also stationed at **Fort Heiman** on the Tennessee River in the Southeast corner of Calloway County, and constituted the left wing of General Nathan B. Forrest, when he made his assault on Johnsonville, Tenn., on November 4th, and 5th, 1864.

The Confederate Seventh Kentucky Infantry Company G was recruited in 1862, and numbered about 65 men. Another Company belonging to the Seventh Regiment was organized in 1862, the original membership was only about 40, over half of whom were killed during the period of their service.

Confederate Col. Faulkner's Cavalry Company G was made up wholly from Calloway County in 1863. It numbered about 80 men, and took part in the western campaign during the later part of the war.

Confederate Captain James Melton raised a Company for the same

Regiment, the greater number of his men being residents of Calloway County. This was a full Company and the majority of the men were under 18 years of age.

Confederate Captain Noah Swann's Company G, C.S.A. became engaged in active conflict within days after organization in the battle of Paris at Paris Tenn. In September 1864, Company C was detached to General Nathan B. Forrest.

Continuous gun and supply running to the southern troops, and occasional small attacks upon Federal steamers moving up the Tennessee River to supply Union troops participating in battles elsewhere in the south caused concern for the Union Army, they were well aware that the area of Calloway County and other surrounding areas were sympathetic to the southern cause.

According to a diary compiled by Josh Ellison in the winter of 1863-64, a squad of Union soldiers came from Paducah to Murray and burned the east side of the court square on Friday night and on Monday night they burned the North side of the square. The Union soldiers also removed from office several county officials who refused to take an oath of allegiance to the Union, many were taken to Paducah and placed in jail. The burning of the East and North sides of the court square was more a reprisal for the majority's sympathy with the C.S.A. than a justifiable act of war. However acts of war are generally condoned by the winners and condemned by the vanquished.#

THE HANGING OF WILLIAM REDWINE ALLBRITTEN

William Redwine Allbritten (married Thomas Burton's sister Elizabeth, also William Redwine's son William R. Allbritten enlisted with Thomas and also mustered into the 13th Tennessee Cavalry)The elder William Redwine was taken out during the last years of the war and hung by guerrilla's. The story goes that William was born in Calloway County in 1824. Married twice, he had 7 children by his first wife, Susan Stubblefield, and 8 by his second wife, Elizabeth (Miss Lizzie) Burton. By thrift and hard work he acquired land, owned a tobacco factory, and ran a General Store in New Providence. He was always busy, saying he had to work in order to leave his family "well-fixed" when he died.

Near the end of the Civil War, Guerrillas roamed the country preying on those left at home during the fighting. They took anything and everything they could lay their hands on. This fall day, two hard-looking men rode to the Allbritten place. Two little girls were making fried pies and getting dinner ready for their father when he came in from the store at noon. Wm. Redwine was grabbed before he got to the house and considerably roughed-up because he refused to say where the valuables were hidden. Being stronger than he was, they dragged him struggling and fighting, threw a rope over a tree limb, and swung him up!

Both guerrillas swaggered into the house trying to scare the girls Sarah Francis and Mary Jane. the girls were spunky, having a hot frying pan of sizzling grease, the other a big-tined fork. So the thieves went on upstairs going through everything, and came down holding their fathers gold watch, which they had found under the mattress. Going to the fireplace, they fingered the bottom of the clock on the mantel (a usual hiding place), and pulled out "Papa's lucky $20 gold piece."

The girls were crying, not being able to do anything to save their father or his valuables. Banging out of the house the guerrillas looked

up at the body swinging from the tree: "Best cut him down. Them lil gals are not strong enough for the job. Seems like he's shore a goner - kicked his shoes off!" Out came a knife to saw through the rope - the body fell with a loud thud, which brought laughs from the hangmen. They mounted their horses and rode away at a gallop.

Calling to their brother, John Calvin, who had been hiding in the attic, they dashed out to bring their father inside. Though John Calvin was a big boy, he was not yet of conscription age. But guerrillas often nabbed such a boy and "sold" him to either side, for a bonus prize.

The three children somehow lifted and dragged their father into the house and onto the front room bed. He was still alive! The cut rope let him drop to the ground and knocked the breath back into his body. He survived, but his recovery was long and slow. He forever had a rope-burn scar which he covered with a scarf till he could grow a beard to cover it.

With the beard, he looked a different person. When the war was over, one day a stranger came into Mr. Allbritten's store. Across his vest hung the fob and watch chain belonging to Wm. Redwine. His watch had to be in that man's pocket! Mr. Allbritten yelled for issom the slave to bring a pitch fork "right quick!" and leaned over grabbing the man and holding on while he rounded the counter. Knocking the man's hat off, he grabbed his hair and beat his head on the counter, giving him a verbal dressing down. He yanked his watch from the alien's pocket, looked it over and placed it where he had always worn it. Justice at last!

He and Issom propelled tha man out the door and gave him a hearty kick into the dusty road where his wagon and team where waiting. Though hurt, this man managed to climb into the wagon and take off, glad to escape with his life.

NOTE:
Wm. Redwine continued to live and work. He died December 5, 1890, a well -liked and well-respected man. "

William Redwine Allbritten

13TH TENNESSEE CAVALRY

Thomas F. Burton accompanied by his brother in law William H. Allbritten, step nephew William R. Allbritten, and neighbor John C. Simmons enlisted into the U.S. Army August 18th 1863. Thomas's younger brother David soon joined him and enlisted on August 26th.

Thomas and the other men volunteered for service into the 13th Tennessee Cavalry Company A, under Captain Theodorick F. Bradford and a 1st LT. John F. Gregory who was commissioned later on October 26th 1863 with all 50 men. Thomas mustered in at the rank of 3rd Sergeant October 21st 1863, David M. Burton mustered in at the rank of Corporal on the same date. John C. Simmons mustered in at the rank of Private on Ocotober 21st. William R. Allbritten mustered in at the rank of corporal on November 18th, and William H. Allbritten musterd in at the rank of Private on November 18th also. Pvt. Carroll Sweeny (pictured) from Smithland Kentucky, mustered into service on August 26th, he was then mustered into Co. A, of the 13th TN Cavalry while in Paducah on October 24th. Company A, was officially mustered into the 13th Tennessee Cavalry on December 5th 1863.

In the winter of 1863-64, Thomas and Company A, was in the New Providence area of Calloway County, Kentucky. While camping nearby Thomas had a opportunity to visit with his family on January 7th 1864 during the birth of his only child. The story that has been past down through the Burton family is as follows, "the 13th Cavalry had camped on Tater Hill in New Providence, directly across from Thomas's house (Present day location of John Burton's house). A doctor M.M. Mason from Henry County Tennessee was present to deliver the new baby. At dark, Maranda's sister Mary Allbritten(Aunt Sis McCuiston) signaled Thomas that the baby had been born by waving a white sheet, it is then said that Thomas was allowed by his superior officer to go in for a brief visit, he walked in the house to see his wife and new son, John Thomas Burton, he was not allowed to stay long and had to leave shortly therafter." This visit would be the last time Maranda and Thomas would ever see each other again.^^

According to Oleta Swift, Thomas's Great Granddaughter it was during this same time that the "rebs" were after the 13th TN. Cavalry, while the "rebs" were traveling down the State Line road a red [Butternut] coat was lost in the road by one of their soldiers, Aunt Sis found the red coat in the road and had taken it home, when she heard the rebel army "a-comin" back, she had taken a broom handle and stuck the coat down in the bottom of a barrel of lye soap that she had made, the lye soap would eat the coat up, were the rebels couldn't find it, if they had they would have killed all three of them (meaning Maranda, her son John, and Aunt Sis).^^

During the winter of 1863 and until the 17th of January 1864 Thomas was stationed at Fort Anderson in Paducah, at this time Fort Anderson was Commanded by Colonel Stephen G. Hicks of the 40th Illinois Infantry. In March 1864 (The 13th TN Cavalry was at Fort Pillow during this time) the Fort consisted of 665 men. Of the 665 men 271 of them belonged to the 16th Kentucky Cavalry, 274 belonged to the Black 1st Kentucky Heavy Artillery, 120 to the 122nd Illinois Infantry.

On January 17th, 1864 as the 13th Tennessee Cavalry Regiment, the Battalion was ordered to report to the Commanding Officer Brigadier General H.T. Reid at Columbus, Kentucky, for duty. Fort Columbus at this time was primarily a supply depot. Here

^^ *Information provided by Oleta Swift-Great Granddaughter.*

they united with Major William F. Bradford and the other Companies of the 13th TN. Cavalry. The 13th TN Cavalry mustered in more men at this time, Sgt. Elburt Jones (pictured) mustered into Co. B, of the 13th TN Cavalry while at Columbus. The 13th Tennessee Cavalry proceeded from this point to Fort Pillow by river boats converted to carry troops and horses.

Sergeant Elbert Jones
13th Tennessee Cavalry Co. B, U.S.

Private Carrol Sweeney
13th Tennessee Cavalry Co. A, U.S.

Private John Simmons
13th Tennessee Cavalry Co. A. U.S.

Charcoal picture of Thomas from the original tin type, Maranda and Thomas's pictures were both done this way, Lula Burton Simmons passed the original charcoal pictures on to her grandaughter Glynda Swift Black.

WILLIAM F. BRADFORDS BATTALION

Thirteenth Tennessee Cavalry
Entire list of men from Bradford's Battalion

Name	Rank	Age	Enlisted	Mustered	Remarks
Company A,					
1. John F Gregory	1st Lt.	24	Oct 26 63	Oct 26 63	Mustered Oct 26 1863 with 50 men: received and accepted commission from Governor Oct 26 1863: went on duty in new grade the same day.
2. George W Craig	1 Ser	28	Aug 19	Oct 21	
3. James B Phipps	QMS	44	Sep 4	Oct 21	
4. William R Fornshee	CSS	18	Oct 10	Oct 21	
5. Randolph C Gunter	1 DS		Nov 20	Nov 20	
6. Steph W Sutterfield	2 DS	26	Oct 6	Oct 21	
7. Thomas F Burton	**3 DS**	**32**	**Aug 18**	**Oct 21**	
8. Nathan C Wiggs	4 DS		Sep 16	Oct 21	
9. Valentia V Matheny	5 DS	18	Nov 9	Nov 18	
10. Wm R Allbritton	Cor	24	Aug 18	Nov 18	Thomas F. Burton's sister Elizabeth's step son by marriage to William Redwine Allbritten
11. Henry H Williams	Cor	23	Aug 22	Oct 26	
12. David M Burton	Cor	21	Aug 26	Oct 21	Thomas F. Burton's Brother
13. Andrew J Glass	Cor		Nov 30	Dec 5	
14. Elijah F Burcham	Cor	24	Oct 10	Oct 21	
15. John W Babb	Cor	21	Aug 18	Oct 21	
16. Thomas J Morgan	Cor	18	Sep 6	Oct 21	
17. Willam H Martin	Cor		Nov 22	Nov 22	
18. Rial D Allen	Bksm	45	Sep 19	Oct 21	
19. Eph L Churchwell	Bksm	27	Nov 19	Nov 19	
20. Thomas J Powell	Wgnr		Nov 22	Nov 22	
21. Anderson Charles	Privt.	35	Oct 2	Oct 21	
22. Anderson Francis	"	31	Oct 20	Oct 21	
23. Arnold Ezekiel	"	33	Aug 24	Aug 26	
24. Allbritton William	"	24	Aug 18	Nov 18	Maranda Burton's Brother
25. Adkinson William	"		Nov 1	Nov 20	
26. Adkinson Richd A	"		Nov 1	Dec 5	
27. Antoine Peter	"		Nov 23	Dec 5	
28. Burcham George W	"		21 Nov	1 Nov 18	
29. Burcham James D	"		Dec 1	Dec 5	
30. Burcham Chris C	"		Nov 30	Dec 5	
31. Burcham John	"		Nov 30	Dec 5	
32. Blelock Robert W	"	41	Nov 8	Nov 18	
33. Bohannon William	"	30	Nov 1	Nov 19	
34. Beckner Isaac	"		Dec 1	Dec 5	
35. Babb George W	"		Nov 25	Dec 5	
36. Cartwright Thos J	"	17	Sep 26	Oct 21	
37. Cooksey Woodford H	"	42	Oct 2	Oct 21	
38. Christenburg Jas M	"	30	Sep 24	Oct 21	
39. Carter William F	"	31	Sep 24	Oct 21	
40. Clark James	"	43	Sep 24	Oct 26	

41. Callison Carrol	Private	19	Nov 1	Nov 18	
42. Childers James C	"		Nov 24	Dec 5	
43. Dunn George H	"		Nov 20	Nov 20	
44. Etter Daniel	"		Dec 1	Dec 5	
45. Frazier William	"		Dec 1	Dec 5	
46. Forrester Josiah M	"	18	Aug 18	Oct 21	
47. Gregory Pitcher H	"	18	Oct 6 1863	Oct 21 1863	
48. Gregory Lynn B	"	20	Sep 8	Oct 21	
49. Gaskins Amos L	"	24	Aug 24	Oct 26	
50. Goodrich William	"		Aug 19	Oct 21	
51. Gooden John	"		Nov 25	Dec 5	
52. Green Joseph M	"		Dec 1	Dec 5	
53. Hardison Thos M	"	19	Oct 5	Oct 21	
54. Hankins Preston	"	32	Sep 16	Oct 21	
55. Heathcot Richard	"	26	Aug 24	Oct 26	
56. Hanwell Jackson T	"	24	Nov 10	Nov 19	
57. Haynes Garrett	"		Nov 22	Nov 22	
58. Halford John	"		Nov 30	Dec 5	
59. Halford Joseph	"		Dec 1	Dec 5	
60. James Joseph	"	18	Oct 2	Oct 26	
61. Knight Andrew J	"		Nov 20	Nov 20	
62. Kirk George W	"		Dec 1	Dec 5	
63. Lydon Micheal	"	27	Aug 18	Oct 21	
64. Long John W	"	21	Sep 5	Oct 21	
65. Lovett William F	"	18	Nov 9	Nov 18	
66. Loftis Thomas	"		Nov 2	Nov 20	
67. Lemmons John E	"		Nov 23	Dec 5	
68. Lindsley James H	"		Nov 30	Dec 5	
69. Mekel Charles W	"	28	Oct 2	Oct 21	
70. Michenor James P	"	18	Sep 24	Oct 21	
71. Miller Benjamin F	"	27	Sep 4	Oct 26	
72. McKenzie Mark	"	18	Sep 4	Oct 26	
73. Mingeor James W	"	18	Aug 31	Oct 21	
74. Meador James P	"	18	Sep 24	Oct 26	
75. Mitchum Marcus	"		Nov 3	Dec 5	
76. Moore James	"		Nov 20	Nov 20	
77. Mitchell James W	"	21	Nov 8	Nov 18	
78. Mathews Sandy	"		Nov 28	Dec 5	
79. McDonald William	"	26	Oct 19	Oct 21	
80. Nelson Robert W	"	22	Aug 19	Oct 21	
81. Nipper Jasper	"	17	Aug 19	Oct 21	
82. Nelson James	"		Nov 23	Dec 5	
83. Norcutt William	"		Nov 30	Dec 5	
84. Nealy James W	"	29	Aug 18	Oct 21	
85. Prince Calvin M	"		Sep 13	Oct 21	
86. Paul Sylvester B	"	19	Nov 8	Nov 18	
87. Park James	"		Nov 24	Dec 5	
88. Robinson Wiley	"	18	Nov 19	Nov 19	
89. Riggs George 3rd	"		Nov 26	Dec 5	
90. Simmons John C	"	25	Aug 18	Oct 21	Thomas F, Burton's neighbor
91. Stafford Samuel S	"		Aug 24	Oct 21	
92. Sweeney Carrol	"	32	Aug 24	Oct 26	Picture enclosed
93. Snead David	"		Nov 24	Dec 5	
94. Taylor Archie F	"		Nov 1	Nov 20	
95. Tatum John B	Private		Nov 28	Dec 5	

96. Taylor William C	"	18	Aug 26	Oct 21	
97. Williams John C	"	25	Sep 23	Oct 21	
98. Wilkins Samuel E	"	20	Sep 26	Oct 21	
99. Wilkins Henry I	"	19	Nov 9	Nov 18	
100. Wallace Charles J	"		Nov 1	Nov 20	
101. White Addison H	"		Nov 30	Dec 5	

Company B,

1. John H Porter	1 Lt	27	Jan 20 64	Jan 20 64	
2. William Cleary	2 Lt	19	Dec 16 63	Dec 16 63	(Took statements)
3. William P Flowers	1 Ser	25	Sept 15	Nov 25	
4. Allen Flowers	QMS	38	Dec 6	Dec 14	
5. Leonidas Guattney	C Ser	39	Dec 1	Dec 14	
6. Milliam A Winn	Sergt	20	Sept 15	Dec 14	(Testified)
7. James W Pulley	Sergt	30	Sept 15	Nov 25	
8. William E Johnson	Sergt	32	Sept 15	Nov 25	
9. James Jones	Sergt	22	Nov 25	Nov 25	
10. Elbert Jones	Sergt	32	Dec 6	Dec 14	Picture enclosed
11. Daniel B Fields	Corp	23	Dec 5	Dec 14	
12. Columbus R Attin	Corp	18	Nov 15	Nov 25	
13. William I Woodward	Corp	25	Nov 23	Nov 25	
14. William Etheridge	Corp	19	Nov 29	Dec 14	
15. George W Weathars	Corp	28	Dec 6	Dec 14	
16. John L S Rodgers	Corp	19	Dec 6	Dec 14	
17. Samuel Morrow	Corp	26	Nov 29	Dec 14	
18. William A Dickey	Corp	27	Dec 1	Dec 14	(Testified)
19. Milas M Deason	Trptr	29	Nov 23	Nov 25	
20. James A Beaty	Trptr	18	Sept 15	Nov 25	
21. Thomas W Avory	Phdis	20	Sept 15	Nov 25	
22. Thomas M Pautk	Phdis	18	Dec 3	Dec 14	
23. Robert M Jones	Sadlr	30	Dec 4	Dec 14	
24. George W Bowels	Wagn	21	Dec 6	Dec 14	
25. Asprey William C	Private	25	Sept 15	Nov 25	
26. Autry John L	"	30	Nov 29	Dec 5	
27. Alexander Francis A	"	39	Nov 21	Nov 25	
28. Allison Benjamin F	"	24	Dec 12	Dec 14	
29. Alexander Doster Z	"	22	Dec 12	Dec 14	
30. Barker Samuel	"	35	Dec 12	Dec 14	
31. Byron John H	"	19	Nov 18	Nov 25	
32. Bailey Anderson	"	18	Nov 23	Nov 25	
33. Bredsoe William J	"	19	Sept 15	Nov 25	
34. Baker Isaac A	"	29	Dec 1	Dec 14	
35. Burris Dempsey	"	30	Dec 5	Dec 14	
36. Burris John	"	19	Dec 2	Dec 14	
37. Byrd Thomas H	"	33	Dec 5	Dec 14	
38. Britts Green L	"	28	Dec 5	Dec 14	
39. Bouls William G	"	26	Dec 6	Dec 14	
40. Bouls Charles F	"	18	Dec 6	Dec 14	
41. Capher John H	"	18	Sept 15	Nov 25	
42. Cochran Ammon H	"	18	Oct 1	Nov 25	
43. Crasby Oaleb	"	27	Dec 1	Dec 14	
44. Crawford Andrew	"	36	Dec 1	Dec 14	
45. Cope William L	"	26	Dec 1	Dec 14	
46. Ellington Richard	"	23	Nov 23	Nov 25	
47. Ellington James M	Private	33	Dec 12	Dec 14	

#	Name	Rank	Age		
48.	Ellington Zachariah	"	18	Dec 11	Dec 14
49.	Eason James D	"	26	Nov 23	Dec 14
50.	Freeman Isaac C W	"	18	Nov 19	Nov 25
51.	Flowers Barney	"	19	Nov 23	Nov 25
52.	Faulkner William J	"	18	Dec 10	Dec 14
53.	Flowers Felix	"	36	Dec 6	Dec 14
54.	Green Benjamin	"	19	Nov 29	Dec 14
55.	Hathway David A	"	18	Sept 15	Nov 25
56.	Hubbs Samuel	"	18	Sept 15	Nov 25
57.	Hosea Jesse B	"	27	Sept 15	Nov 25
58.	Hott Joseph P	"	18	Sept 10	Nov 25
59.	Hauser William T	"	19	Dec 6	Dec 14
60.	James William	"	36	Nov 23 63	Dec 14 63
61.	Jackson Burton	"	19	Dec 5	Dec 14
62.	King Rufus E	"	33	Dec 6	Dec 14
63.	Lanier William H	"	25	Nov? 15	Nov 28
64.	Lonan Jason	"	18	Nov 15	Nov 28
65.	Little Charles I	"	18	Oct 25	Nov 28
66.	Leonard David H	"	23	Dec 5	Dec 14
67.	Mifflin William	"	19	Sept 15	Nov 25
68.	McQuester Randle P	"	18	Oct 25	Nov 25
69.	Michaels Alfred	"	23	Dec 11	Dec 14
70.	McKee Andrew	"	34	Dec 1	Dec 14
71.	Morrow John W	"	26	Dec 5	Dec 14
72.	Pope Lewis D	"	23	Nov 19	Nov 25
73.	Porter Pinkney	"	18	Nov 19	Nov 25
74.	Pankey Samuel	"	18	Nov 25	Nov 25
75.	Peck Francis M	"	18	Nov 15	Nov 25
76.	Perry Thomas L	"	18	Oct 8	Nov 25
77.	Pruett Garrett	"	26	Dec 6	Dec 14
78.	Ray John F.				(Testified)
79.	Ray Samuel	"	18	Nov 11	Nov 25
80.	Ray George H	"	24	Dec 1	Dec 14
81.	Reager Robert W	"	27	Dec 6	Dec 14
82.	Redford James H	"	44	Dec 6	Dec 14
83.	Stayton John W	"	19	Sept 15	Nov 25
84.	Sanders George R	"	19	Sept 15	Nov 25
85.	Short William	"	20	Sept 15	Nov 25
86.	Sloan James D	"	19	Nov 1	Nov 25
87.	Stout Levi J	"	20	Sept 10	Nov 25
88.	Stout James H F	"	18	Oct 22	Nov 25
89.	Smothers John W	"	25	Sept 15	Nov 25
90.	Scoby Peter L	"	22	Dec 1	Dec 14
91.	Scoby John A H	"	21	Dec 1	Dec 14
92.	Stephens William J	"	37	Dec 5	Dec 14
93.	Smith Samuel E	"	20	Dec 2	Dec 14
94.	Taylor John	"	28	Dec 12	Dec 14
95.	Tilghman Robert C	"	34	Nov 24	Nov 25
96.	Tilghman Joshua C	"	21	Nov 24	Nov 25
97.	Tilghman Pinkney	"	32	Nov 24	Nov 25
98.	Thompson Franklin	"	39	Dec 1	Dec 14
99.	Wells John	"	19	Sept 15	Nov 25
100.	Winn James A	"	22	Sept 15	Nov 25
101.	Woodward Stephen D	Private	20	Nov 23	Nov 25
102.	Wilson James M	"	21	Oct 1	Nov 25

103.Williams William J   "   29   Dec 12   Dec 14

Company C,

# Name	Rank	Age			Notes
1. Nicholas D Logan	1 Lt.		Dec 16 63	Dec 16 63	Received and accepted commission from Gover nor of Tenn Dec 16 1863: went on duty in new grade same day.
2. Herbert A Henry	OrSer		20 Oct	1 Dec 14	
3. John A Clock	QMS	22	Sept 6	Dec 14	
4. James H Webb C	Ser	19	Nov 29	Dec 14	
5. Wm B Lursley	Sergt	19	Dec 3	Dec 21	
6. David Shaw	Sergt	24	Nov 1	Dec 14	
7. Isaiah Hogan	Sergt	22	Dec 3	Dec 14	
8. Alfred Medelton	Sergt	39	Dec 2	Dec 14	
9. George L Ellis	Sergt	20	Nov 28	Dec 14	
10. John H Gales	Corpl	18	Oct 25	Dec 14	
11. Benj W Lancaster	Corpl	20	Nov 27	Dec 14	
12. Benj F Roach	Corpl	18	Nov 30	Dec 19	
13. Joseph H Bunch	Corpl	20	Nov 29	Dec 14	
14. Wm A Rider	Corpl	21	Sept 1	Dec 14	
15. Joseph Norman	Corpl	37	Dec 15	Dec 15	
16. Jas H McDonald	Corpl	20	Dec 19	Dec 19	
17. Wm Mouldin	Corpl	21	Dec 14	Dec 21	
18. Jos M Nichols	Trptr	18	Nov 28	Dec 14	
19. Thomas Wheelis	Trptr	18	Sept 1	Dec 14	
20. Thos E Needham	Far'r	23	Nov 17	Jan 8 64	
21. Phillip Oxford	Far'r	21	Dec 28	Jan 8 64	
22. George Dutton	Sadlr	19	Dec 28	Jan 8 64	
23. Francis M Gammons	Wgnr	19	Nov 24	Dec 14 63	
24. Bancom Wm A	Private	39	Dec 1	Dec 14	
25. Bowles Wm H	"	18	Sept 15	Dec 14	
26. Box George	"	25	Dec 1	Dec 14	
27. Crews Wm S	"	32	Dec 22	Jan 8 64	
28. Casey Elisha	"	20	Oct 24	Dec 20 63	
29. Collins Frank	"	20	Dec 9	Dec 14	
30. Campbell Helm	"	23	Nov 25	Dec 14	
31. Cornish Alderson	"	18	Sept 1	Dec 14	
32. Tate Wm L	"	32	Dec 17	Jan 8 64	
33. Dunegan Thomas	"	21	Dec 2	Dec 14 63	
34. Dupree Daniel C	"	22	Dec 5	Dec 5	
35. Day Martin V	"	18	Oct 24	Dec 14	
36. Gateswood John	"	18	Dec 7	Dec 14	
37. Garrison James M	"	20	Dec 13	Dec 14	
38. Hazlebrigg Andrew	"	31	Dec 14	Dec 15	
39. Heinrichs Henry C	"	20	Dec 29	Jan 8 64	
40. Heinrichs Gilbert W	"	30	Dec 29	Jan 8 64	
41. Henline Summerf'd	"	18	Jan 8 64	Jan 8 64	
42. Henline Geo T	"	25	Jan 8 64	Jan 8 64	
43. Henderson Natha'l G	"	40	Dec 7 63	Dec 21 63	
44. Hall James E	"	19	Oct 26	Dec 14	
45. Hammonds Jessie W	Private	28	Dec 2	Dec 14	
46. Ham James	"	24	Dec 14	Dec 14	
47. Ham Lue	"	22	Dec 14	Dec 14	
48. Jones John	"	39	Dec 1	Dec 14	

49. Kelso Frederick	"	18	Oct 18	Dec 14	
50. McGee Alexander	"	31	Dec 5	Dec 14	
51. McMitchell Jas W	"	21	Dec 20	Jan 8 64	
52. McMitchell Wm L	"	20	Sept 20	Dec 17 63	
53. Myers Andrew McDonald	"	18	Dec 15	Jan 4 64	
54. McDonald Robert D	"	18	Dec 19	Dec 19 63	
55. Morris Henry S	"	19	Nov 27	Dec 14	
56. Miller Abraham	"	35	1863	Dec 14 1863	
57. Mitchell Jones M	"	23	Dec 2	Dec 14	
58. McGlaughlin Jno M	"	21	Sept 14	Oct 21	
59. Nunemaker Daniel	"	19	Nov 9	Nov 18	
60. Oliver Lewis H	"	26	Dec 2	Dec 29	
61. Price Wm F	"	19	Nov 18	Nov 20	
62. Parks Jesse	"	38	Nov 3	Dec 14	
63. Poach Samuel M	"	26	Dec 15	Dec 19	
64. Rasberry Lott G	"	28	Jan 9 64	Jan 11 64	
65. Reger Washington L	"	25	Dec 14 63	Jan 8 64	
66. Rice Jas T	"	19	Dec 6 63	Jan 8 64	
67. Rankin Daniel H	"	19	Nov 23 63	Jan 8 64	(Testified)
68. Rogers Berry I	"	28	Sept 1 63	Jan 8 64	
69. Ruffins Thomas	"	29	Nov 27 63	Jan 8 64	
70. Scarborough Edw'd	"	19	Sept 20 63	Jan 8 64	
71. Scoby Joseph R	"	18	Nov 29 63	Dec 17 63	
72. Southerton Jasper	"	32	Dec 1	Dec 14	
73. Stafford John	"	34	Dec 13	Dec 14	
74. Stafford Wm P	"	24	Dec 13	Dec 14	
75. Stafford James	"	18	Dec 13	Dec 14	
76. Smith James A	"	22	Sept 18	Dec 14	
77. Tidwell John W	"	18	Dec 9	Dec 14	
78. Taylor John C	"	20	Dec 3	Dec 14	
79. Viah Simpson H	"	21	Dec 19	Dec 20	
80. Vaught Leander C	"	46	Dec 17	Dec 20	
81. Ward Thomas I	"	18	Jan 1 64	Jan 8 64	
82. Wright Gideon H	"	21	Dec 19 63	Dec 19 63	
83. Wright James	"	25	Dec 8	Dec 18	

Company D,

1. Francis A Smith	1 Lt	39	Dec 16 63	Dec 16 63	Received and accepted commission Dec 16 1863 from Governor of Tenn: went on duty in new grd same day wh 50 men 2.
2. John C Barr	2 Lt	27	Jan 20 64	Jan 20 64	Promoted from privt Co L 15 Ill, to Vol Cav by Governor of Tenn.
3. Isaiah Jones	1 Ser	31	Dec 5 63	Jan 14 64	Received and acceted commision Jan 20 1864: went on duty in new grd same day.
4. John Jackson	Q M S	35	Dec 9 63	Jan 14 64	
5. Jones A Talley	C Ser	40	Dec 2	Jan 14	
6. John K Kate	Serg.	20	Dec 9	Jan 14	
7. William P Stephens	Serg.	24	Dec 7	Jan 14	
8. Wm P Walker	Serg.	21	Dec 1	Jan 14	
9. Robert S Kendall	Serg.	35	Nov 29	Jan 14	

10. Elam V Cashion	Serg.	22	Dec 9	Jan 14
11. Hughey W Poyles	Corp.	27	Dec 12	Jan 14
12. Wm A Nicholson	Corp.	28	Dec 9	Jan 14
13. James D Dollins	Corp.	35	Nov 30	Jan 14
14. Michael Click	Corp.	36	Dec 2	Jan 14
15. Phillip S Scott	Corp.	31	Dec 1	Jan 14
16. John H Jones	Corp.	20	Dec 6	Jan 14
17. Benj R Chambers	Corp.	23	Nov 26	Jan 14
18. Paton A Alexander	Corp.	40	Dec 9	Jan 14
19. Francis M Pankey	Trptr	24	Nov 26	Jan 14
20. Edward Steward	Trptr	18	Nov 24	Jan 14
21. William M Masters	F Blk	32	Dec 1	Jan 14
22. Benjamin F Hawkins	F Blk	20	Nov 30	Jan 14
23. James A Donnell	Sadlr	34	Dec 12	Jan 14
24. Richard Landrum	Wagnr	20	Dec 13	Jan 14
25. Brown James M	Private	27	Dec 2	Jan 14
26. Brock Henry M	"	29	Dec 12	Dec 19 63
27. Busby John	"	34	Jan 1 64	Jan 8 64
28. Burnett Benjamin F	"	23	Dec 1 63	Dec 14 63
29. Carpenter Albert FM	"	30	Dec 12	Dec 19
30. Crawford George W	"	18	Dec 5	Dec 14
31. Cloys Hiram O	"	30	Dec 1	Dec 14
32. Cloys Francis M	"	34	Dec 1	Dec 14
33. Cloys Marcus C	"	32	Dec 1	Dec 14
34. Crockett Robert B	"	31	Jan 6 64	Jan 8 64
35. Davis William P	"	40	Dec 4 63	Dec 14 63
36. Dawtry Samuel	"	33	Jan 1 64	Jan 8 64
37. Easterwood John W	"	25	Dec 10 63	Dec 14 63
38. Elks John W	"	27	Jan 1 64	Jan 8 64
39. Floyd Daniel	"	28	Dec 4 63	Dec 17 63
40. Foulks Nathan G	"	44	Dec 1	Dec 14
41. Green Joseph C	"	18	Dec 1	Dec 14
42. Gibson James W	"	28	Jan 6 64	Jan 8 64
43. Harrison David W	"	31	Dec 11 63	Dec 14 63
44. Haisless Laton	"	28	Dec 5	Dec 14
45. Hopper Daniel M	"	19	Dec 3	Dec 14
46. Hester James T	"	35	Dec 26	Jan 8 64
47. Hutchens Charles	"	32	Dec 22	Jan 8
48. Hugneley Charles W	"	30	Dec 22	Jan 8
49. Hugneley Samuel E	"	27	Dec 22	Jan 8
50. Jones Lewis H	"	30	Dec 5	Dec 14 63
51. Johnson Briant	"	24	Dec 4	Dec 14
52. Johnson William R	"	23	Nov 30	Dec 14
53. King Benjamin W	"	22	Dec 4	Dec 14
54. Kirk Sydney E	"	18	Dec 9	Dec 14
55. Kirk Bunyon J	"	21	Dec 9	Dec 14
56. Key Franklin A	"	31	Dec 5	Dec 14
57. Landrum James W	"	32	Dec 12	Dec 15
58. Miller Samuel N	"	34	Dec 5	Dec 14
59. Moore Andrew J	Private	21	Dec 3	Dec 14
60. Moutrie William L	"	20	Jan 6 64	Jan 8 1864
61. McConnell John C	"	29	Dec 12 63	Dec 14 63
62. Neiley John D	"	20	Dec 11	Dec 14
63. Neily Hiram S	"	26	Dec 12	Dec 14
64. Paschal Thaddeus	"	20	Dec 5	Dec 14

65. Pickens James D	"	21	Dec 9	Dec 14
66. Pickens Newton P	"	18	Dec 17	Dec 19
67. Rummage Jefferson	"	25	Dec 9	Dec 14
68. Read William B	"	27	Dec 5	Dec 14
69. Smith Aaron P	"	25	Dec 10	Dec 14
70. Smith William J	"	24	Dec 9	Dec 14
71. Smith Levi	"	31	Dec 4	Dec 18
72. Stewart James C	"	23	Jan 8 64	Jan 8 64
73. Scofy David J	"	20	Dec 1 63	Dec 17 63
74. Scofy Wiley B	"	23	Dec 22	Jan 8 64
75. Self Samuel J	"	26	Dec 26	Jan 8 64
76. Tidwell Franklin D	"	18	Dec 1	Dec 14 63
77. Thompson Thomas J	"	40	Dec 1	Dec 14
78. Underwood Benjamin F	"	35	Dec 1	Dec 14
79. Waters John A	"	27	Dec 2	Dec 14
80. Walker William P.				(Testified)
81. Webb Samuel J	"	26	Jan 1 64	Jan 8 64
82. Wiggs Jonathan S	"	31	Dec 22 63	Jan 8
83. Williams William F	"	28	Dec 1	Dec 14 63 (Wife testified)
84. Wilson Jonathan	"	45	Oct 21	Dec 14
85. Wright William A	"	42	Jan 6 64	Jan 8 64

Company E,
1. Daniel Stamps   (Testified)
2. James N. Taylor   (Testified)

MEMORANDA

A Battalion of Cavalry was raised by Major W.F. Bradford in December, 1863, and January, 1864, consisting of four Companies, and organized at Union City, Tenn. It was first incorrectly designated the 13th Cavalry. The following orders and report gives its history. After the Fort Pillow Battle Company A, on the 14th of February, 1865, consolidated with the 6th Tennessee Cavalry, by an order from the Adjutant General's office, and was known as Company E.

ADJUTANT GENERAL'S OFFICE, STATE OF TENNESSEE,

Nashville, Aug. 18th, 1864.
General Order No. 13 } Extract.
Companies A,B, C and D of a Battalion of Tennessee Cavalry, organized by Major W.F. Bradford, and erroneously designated the 13th Regiment Tennessee Cavalry, and as such mustered into the United States service for the term of three years, by Lieut. George W. Tetterman, 15th U.S. Infantry, A.C.M., 6th Division, 16th A.C., as follows: Company A, Dec 5, 1863; Company B, Dec 16th, 1863; Companies C and D, Jan. 20, 1864; having been reduced below the minimum required for two Companies by killed and taken prisoners at Fort Pillow, Tenn., are hereby consolidated and will be known as a part of the 14th Regiment Tennessee Cavalry. The organization thus formed by the consolidation of the Companies as above named will be designated as Company A.
By order of Brigadier General ANDREW JOHNSON,
Military Governor of Tennessee.
(Signed,) Edward S. Richards, Asst. Adj. Gen.

HEADQUARTERS 14TH REGIMENT TENNESSEE CAVALRY,

Tennessee Barracks, Nashville, January 1, 1865.

Capt. Edward S. Richards,

Asst. Adjt. General of Tennessee, Nashville:

Captain:-In accordance with instructions contained in a circular issued from the Adjutant General's office of the State of Tennessee, bearing date November 1, 1864, I have the honor herewith to submit the following report of the fourteenth Regiment Cavalry of Tennessee Volunteers:

This Regiment, formerly erroneously designated the Thirteenth Regiment, was recruited and organized into a Battalion of four Companies at Union City, and mustered into the United States service on the 26th day of December, 1863, commanded by Major William F. Bradford. It remained at Union City chiefly engaged in recruiting and scouting the surrounding country until the 3d day of February, 1864, when it received orders from Brigadier General W.S. Smith, then Chief of Cavalry of the Military Division of the Mississippi, to establish its headquarters at Fort Pillow, Tennessee, where it was ordered to use all diligence in recruiting and mounting. For the latter purpose we were authorized to impress horses from both the loyal and disloyal, giving vouchers only to those who might furnish unmistakable evidence of their loyalty to the Government of the United States. In pursuance of these orders and instructions from the Chief of Cavalry of the Military Division of the Mississippi, we took up our line of march on the 4th of February, 1864, via the Mobile and Ohio Railroad, to Columbus, Ky., (Thomas Burton and the others with him who mustered into Company A, traveled from Paducah, Ky. to Columbus, Ky. and met up with the recruits from Union City at this point in time) and from thence they traveled down the Mississippi River to Fort Pillow, Tenn., where we arrived on the evening of the 8th of February, 1864.

Recruiting at this point for various reasons, did not progress as rapidly as was first anticipated, and it was not until the 1st of April following that our fifth Company, under command of Capt. Poston, was ready for muster into the United States service. Repeated applications were made to the Major General commanding at Memphis to have a mustering officer sent to perform muster, but for some cause unknown to the authorities at Fort Pillow no officer could be sent for that purpose. At length a representation of these facts was made to Brigadier General R.P. Brickland, then commanding District of Memphis, and an order from him was obtained to take the Company to Memphis for the purpose of there being mustered into the service. However, At the time the order was received, which was on or about the 10th of April, Fort Pillow was being threatened by the enemy under Forrest, and at the request of Major L.F. Booth, 6th U.S. Heavy Artillery, C.T., then Commanding Post, it remained to assist in the defense of the Fort, when two days afterwards, viz: on the 12th of April, it was nearly annihilated, together with the other four Companies, in the heartsickening butchery of our soldiers after the capture of the works by the enemy. With the capture of Fort Pillow terminates the history of this Battalion. Hardly a nucleus of the command remained after the vengeance of the rebel soldiery had been wreaked upon the brave but overpowered defenders of our flag. For ten long hours they held out against overwhelming numbers of the enemy, all the while sending death and destruction into their ranks, and repelling with terrible slaughter their repeated charges. With every temporary advantage thus obtained, cheer after cheer was sent up by the brave "boys in blue" as they beheld with infinite delight the rebel horde recoiling in confusion before their directed fire. Finally, at about four o'clock P.M., the enemy through a violation of his flag of truce, succeeded in overpowering the garrison and compelling it to surrender. Up to this juncture only three of our officers who participated in the fight had fallen, but after the blood-thirsty barbarity of the rebels had been dealt out to their unarmed and helpless prisoners, only three of our officers were found to be alive. These were Lieut. Porter, Lieut. Logan and myself, the Adjutant of the Regiment. Lieutenants Porter and Logan soon after died, the former from his wounds and the latter by reason of his base treatment in prison at Macon, Ga. As for myself, I received a severe wound (at first considered mortal) in my right side, and it was only after several months of the most extreme pain and suffering, that I was enabled to report for duty. The little detachment of men, who, at the time of the fight, were absent from the several companies on duty, were, on the 18th day of August, 1864, consolidated into one company, per General Order No. 13, Adjutant General's office, State of Tennessee, which company by same order, was designated as Company A, of the Fourteenth Regiment of Tennessee Cavalry. In this connection it may not be improper to state that up to this time, our Battalion had been known and it seems in some way, erroneously designated as the Thirteenth West Tennessee Cavalry. The Company commanded by Capt. John L. Poston is now stationed at the Tennessee Barracks in this city. Other regiments have been more fortunate, and as a consequence, have made a more extended record for themselves and the State; but none have borne themselves with more determined spirit of courage and bravery, a truer and more patriotic devotion to their country, or, in short, have won more brilliant record than our Battalion at Fort Pillow.

I am, Captain, very respectfully; your obedient servant,

MACK J. LEAMING,

Lieut. and Adjutant 14th Reg't Tenn. Cavalry.

FORT PILLOW

In January 1864 a portion of the 13th Regiment, under Lieutenant Major William Bradford, was reported to be in Union City, Tennessee, under Colonel Isaac R. Hawkins.

On February 3rd, 1864, while in Union City, Major Bradford Commanding the 13th Tennessee Cavalry, received the following orders from Brig. Gen., William Sooey Smith.

Memphis, Tenn Feb. 1, 1864

Major BRADFORD,
Commanding Thirteenth Tennessee Cavalry:

Sir: All the Cavalry of the department of the Tennessee having been turned over to my command, by order of Major General Sherman, commanding the department, you are hereby ordered to establish yourself for the present at Fort Pillow, on the Mississippi River, and make that your recruiting rendezvous for the present. You will take a good defensible position for your camp, taking advantage of any entrenchment's that may already exist, and constructing any that may be necessary.

You will scout the surrounding country thoroughly as far to the rear as you may deem it safe to take your command, making every effort in your power to hunt up and destroy guerrilla parties. You will subsist your command upon the country as far is possible, and take stock necessary to keep it well mounted, giving vouchers to loyal men only.

Keep your command in condition for active service at all times, drawing arms, ammunition, and equipment's from ordinance department at this city. Use all diligence to recruit your regiment rapidly, and apply to the chief commissary of musters, stationed here, to muster your men promptly.
WN. Sooey Smith
Brig. Gen., Chief of Cavalry, Mil. Div. of the Miss.

Special Field Orders No. 6 }   HDQRS. Sixteenth Army Corps,
                                    Vicksburg, Miss., February 2, 1864
1. Major W.F. Bradford, commanding Thirteenth Cavalry Volunteers, will immediately upon receipt of this order, move his entire command to occupy Fort Pillow, reporting to Brig. Gen. R.P. Buckland, commanding District of Memphis.

All orders from the O.R. Series 1 Volume 31

Union City, February 3, 1864
Brig. Gen., H.T. REID,
Commanding District of Columbus:

Sir: Major Bradford, Thirteenth Tennessee, has this day received orders from General Smith, Chief of Cavalry, to move with his entire force to Fort Pillow, and expects to start to-morrow. I have a party of 60 men scouring east and north of Dresden; will have to furnish guard for railroad train. Under the circumstances, would it not be best for bridges between this place and Columbus to be guarded by troops from the latter place?
Isaac R. Hawkins
Colonel, Commanding Post.

Adjutant Mack J. Leaming reported that the Thirteenth Tennessee Cavalry reached Fort Pillow on February 8th 1864.

In March, Major Bradford sent the following correspondence to Brigadier. Gen., BRAYMEN Commanding Cairo.

HEADQUARTERS POST,
Fort Pillow, Tenn., March 23, 1864.
Brigadier-General BRAYMEN,
Commanding District of Cairo:

General: I have just received reliable information confirming previous information that Forrest, with from 3,000 to 8,000 men, was at Jackson, Tenn., on Monday, 21st instant, and has given orders for the cooking of five days' rations; that Faulkner, with from 600 to 1,200 men was at Wellwood on Tuesday, 22nd instant, 15 miles east of Brownsville, and was also having five days' rations cooked up. The current rumor in their camps was that Forrest intended a raid into Kentucky and was to meet Morgan at some point on the Tennessee River. There was also a report that Faulkner did not have all his men with him, not being able to mount them. The men were not permitted to scatter, but were kept close at camp.

Richardson was reported in the rear with 1,500 men, and would perhaps take Brownsville, Tenn., in his route. They were badly clothed and badly mounted, but seemed to be in buoyant spirits.

I have the honor to be, general, very respectfully, your obedient servant,
W.F. BRADFORD,
Major, Commanding Post.
Bradford report from the O.R. Series 1 Volume 31

HEADQUARTERS SIXTEENTH ARMY CORPS,
Memphis, Tenn., March 28, 1864.
Maj. W.F. BRADFORD,
Thirteenth Tennessee Cavalry:

Major: I send to Fort Pillow four companies colored artillery, who are also drilled as infantry, and two 12-pounder howitzers.

These are good troops, well tried and commanded by a good officer.

Major Booth ranks you and will take command. He has full instructions in writing, which he will show you. I think these troops had better hold the Forts, while yours are held for exterior garrison. In case of attack, you will of course seek refuge in the fortifications.

Keep yourself well posted as to what is going on in the country and keep me advised. I doubt if Forrest will risk himself in the pocket between the Hatchie and Forked Deer, but he may try it. At all events, with 700 good men, your post can be held until assistance arrives.

Your obedient servant,
S.A. HURLBUT,
Major-General.

As of April 1, 1864 the following list contains details of the Thirteenth Cavalry's strength, before Booth arrived to take command.

Fort Pillow (Major William F. Bradford)
9 Officers
262 Enlisted men of the 13th TN Cavalry
329 Aggregate present (58 Civilians)
466 Aggregate present and absent
2 Brass 6 pounder field artillery pieces (cannons)

Strength after Booth arrived to take command.

Fort Pillow (Major L.F. Booth)
10 Officers
278 Enlisted men of the 13th TN Cavalry
292 Elisted men of the 6th Heavy Artillary Colored Regiment and of the
2nd U.S. Light Artillary, Colored regiment.
100 Civilians or more including women and children who had taken refuge
inside the fort to escape conscription.
(Information from N.B.Forrest)
2 10 pounder parrott guns (cannons)
2 12 pounder howitzers (cannons)
2 Brass 6 pounder field artillary pieces (cannons)

HEADQUARTERS SIXTEENTH ARMY CORPS,
Memphis, Tenn., March 28, 1864
Maj. L.F. Booth,
Comdg. First Battalion, First Alabama Siege Artillery:

Sir: You will proceed with your own battalion to Fort Pillow and establish your force in garrison of the works there. As you will be, if I am correct in my memory, the senior officer at that post, you will take command, conferring, however, freely and fully with Major Bradford, Thirteenth Tennessee Cavalry, whom you will find a good officer, though not of much experience.

There are two points of land fortified at Fort Pillow, one of which only is now held by our troops. You will occupy both, either with your own troops alone or holding one with yours and giving the other in charge of Major Bradford. The positions are commanding, and can be held by a small force against almost any odds.

I shall send you at this time two 12-pounder howitzers, as I hope it will not be necessary to mount heavy guns. You will, however, immediately examine the ground and the works, and if, in your opinion, 20-pounder parrotts can be advantageously used, I will order them for you.(These guns were requested by Booth, Hurlbut sent two 10 pounder parrott guns instead and delivered them to Booth before April 12th). My opinion is that there is not range enough. Major Bradford is well acquainted with the country, and should keep scouts well out, and forward all information received direct to me.

I think Forrest's check at Paducah will not dispose him to try the river again, but that he will fall back to Jackson and thence cross the Tennessee; as soon as this is ascertained I shall withdraw your garrison. Nevertheless, act promptly in putting the works into perfect order and post into its strongest defense. Allow as little intercourse as possible with the country, and cause all supplies which go out to be examined with great strictness. No man whose loyalty is questionable should be allowed to come in or go out while the enemy is in West Tennessee.

Your obedient servant,

S.A. HURLBUT,

Major-General.

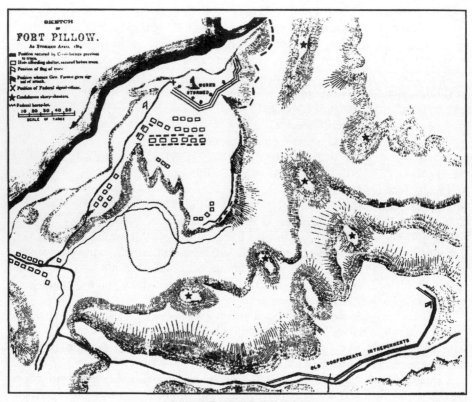

MAP OF FORT PILLOW

Fort Pillow was constructed in 1861 and 1862 by Confederate Gideon Pillow. Over-looking the Mississippi River, it is positioned on one of the Chickasaw Bluffs sixty miles North of Memphis.

HEADQUARTERS, FORT PILLOW,
Fort Pillow, Tenn., April 3, 1864
Major-General HURLBUT:
GENERAL:

Everything seems to be very quiet within a radius of from 30 to 40 miles around, and I do not think any apprehensions need be felt or fears entertained in reference to this place being attacked or even threatened. I think it perfectly safe.

I have the honor to be, general, very respectfully, your obedient servant,
L.F. BOOTH,
Major Sixth U.S. Heavy Artillery (colored), Comdg. Fort.

Ironically, the day after Booth had written Major-General Hurlbut, Forrest had written to Lieutenant-General Polk that he was holding all of Kentucky and Tennessee lying between the Mississippi and Tennessee rivers, and that he had planned on attacking at least one fort on the Mississippi river: "There is a Federal force of 500 or 600 at Fort Pillow, which I will attend to in a day or two, as they have horses and supplies which we need.

It was well known around the Fort Pillow area that the men of the 13th TN Cavalry consisted of men from West Tennessee and West Kentucky, the local southern loyalist considered these men to be traitors or as Nathan Forrest put it "Tennessee Tories", to them these men were worse than Yankee's, and they could not comprehend why Forrest allowed them to remain at Fort Pillow unscathed.

William Bradford, a West Tennessee attorney born in Forrest's native Bedford County, was particularly unpopular. He had orders from Brigadier General William Sooey Smith to scout the surrounding country, hunt up and destroy guerrilla parties, scour the country for recruits and to confiscate stock and supplies that he would need to mount and subsist his command upon the country, he was ordered to give vouchers to loyal men only.

Nathan Bedford Forrest

Locals claimed that Bradfords detachments took horses, mules, beef cattle, beds, plates, wearing apparel, money, and every possible movable article of value, from anyone who could not provide proof of loyalty to the Union.

Bradfords orders to confiscate horses, livestock, etc. as was needed from loyal and un-loyal civilians naturally caused deep resentment.

The hatred of Major Bradford and his men resulted in Southern accusations of physical mistreatment and sexual assault, these accusations began to surface and find its way to Forrest's Command.

33

A delegation of West Tennesseans had made a special trip to visit Forrest, they had come with a petition in hand, this petition included accusations of the previously mentioned and pleaded that Forrest remove the Federals from Fort Pillow immediately.

Many of Forrest's officers begged to be permitted to remain to protect their families from Bradford and his Battalion at Fort Pillow. Forrest was in need of horses, weapons, and supplies, but more importantly, he had become aware that if he didn't remove the Federal soldiers from Fort Pillow, his credibility would be damaged, and the future conscription of soldiers from that part of the state would be almost impossible. Forrest would take Fort Pillow and soon.

In obedience to orders from Major-General Forrest, Brigadier General James R. Chalmers of Mississippi had assumed command of a division composed of McCulloch's brigade of his division and Tyree H. Bell's brigade of Buford's division. On the mourning of April 11th, he moved this division from Sharons Ferry, on Forked Deer, in the direction of Brownsville, and on the same mourning moved Lieutenant-Colonel Chalmers battalion through Brownsville on the Memphis road, and thence circuitous route back again to the Fort Pillow road. Brigadier General Chalmers moved from Brownsville in person, at 3:30 p.m., on the 11th and he reached Fort Pillow, a distance of 40 miles through a pouring rain, at daylight on the mourning of April 12th, 1864, exactly three years to the day that Fort Sumter was fired upon and the Civil War began.

Chalmers was fortunate in securing as a guide Mr. W.J. Shaw, a local citizen who had been recently arrested and confined inside the fort by Major Bradford. Shaw escaped on the 11th, during his confinement he had become very familier with the layout of the fort and the number of troops and artillary that Booth and Bradford commanded.

At about 6 a.m. Colonel McCulloch, commanding advance, surprised the enemy's pickets and captured 4 of them. Federal skirmishers from the 13th Tennessee Cavalry U.S. Companies D, and E, were thrown out to ascertain the position and number of the enemy, the skirmishing lasted about one hour, when the Federal skirmishers were gradually driven back toward the fort on the bluff. It was during this time that Federals Lieutenant Barr and Lieutenant Wilson, latter of the Thirteenth Cavalry were killed outside the fort.

Brigadier General James R. Chalmers

Brigadier General A. Buford

Colonel Robert McCulloch

Brigadier General Tyree H. Bell,
Commanding Bell's Brigade

Back in Memphis, Major-General Hulrbut was notified of the attack on Fort Pillow, he would send the following orders in an attempt to help re-enforce the garrison:

HEADQUARTERS SIXTEENTH ARMY CORPS,
Memphis, Tenn., April 12, 1864 - 7 p.m.
Brig. Gen. R.P. Buckland,
Comdg. District of Memphis, Memphis, Tenn.:
   General: You will send with all possible dispatch a good regiment, with four days rations and full supply of ammunition, to re-enforce Fort Pillow. They will embark at the earliest moment on the steamer "Glendale", or such other boat as may be furnished by the quartermaster's department.
   Promptness is all important.
S.A. Hurlburt,
Major-General.

HEADQUARTERS DISTRICT OF MEMPHIS,
Memphis, Tenn., April 12, 1864.
Col. I.G. Kappner:
   Sir: You will send with all possible dispatch the Fifty-Fifth United States (colored), with four days rations, or as much as they can carry in their haversacks, to re-enforce Fort Pillow. The men will take 40 rounds of ammunition in cartridge-boxes, and you will send 100 rounds extra on wagons to the boat. They will embark at the earliest moment on the steamer "Glendale", or such other boat as may be furnished by Quartermaster's Department. Promptness is all important.
   By order of Brigadier-General Buckland:
   Alf. G. Tuther,
   Captain and acting Assistant Adjutant-General.

HEADQUARTERS SIXTEENTH ARMY CORPS,
Memphis, Tenn., April 12, 1864.
OFFICER COMMANDING FORCE FOR FORT PILLOW:
(Through Brigd. Gen. R.P. Buckland):

Colonel: You will proceed as rapidly as possible by steamer to Fort Pillow and re-enforce the garrison there. With this addition, and the great natural strength of the place, you should be able to hold it. Two gun-boats will be there, with whom you will communicate before landing. Immediately upon landing ascertain as nearly as you can from Major Booth the precise state of affairs, and send a report to cairo and here.

If you find on approaching Fort Pillow that it has unfortunately been taken, you will request the officer of the gun-boat to reconnoiter as closely as possible, and develope some accurate idea of the strength of the enemy, and return. If you succeed in re-enforcing the fort in time it must be held at all hazards and to the last man. Report immediately and by every boat that passes.

Your obedient servant,
S.A. Hurlbut,
Major-General.

Confederate Brigadier-General Chalmers orders from General Forrest were to invest the place, and he proceeded to do as follows: McCulloch's brigade moved down the Fulton road to Gaine's farm; thence north to the fort on a road running parallel with the Mississippi River; Wilson's regiment, of Bell's brigade, moved on the direct road from Brownsville to Fort Pillow, and Colonel Bell with Barteu's and Russell's regiments moved down Coal creek to attack the fort in the rear.

The works at Fort Pillow consisted of a strong line of fortifications, originally constructed by Brigadier-General Pillow, of the C.S. Army, stretching from Coal creek bottom, on the left, to the Mississippi river on the right, in length about 2 miles and at an average distance of about 600 yards from the river. Inside of this outer line and about 600 yards from it stood an interior work on the crest of a commanding hill, originally commenced by Brigadier-General Villepigue, C.S. Army, which covered about 2 acres of ground. About 300 yards in rear of this, above the junction of Coal creek and the Mississippi river, stood the last fortification, which was a strong dirt fort in semicircular form, with a ditch in front of it 12 feet wide and 8 feet deep.

As the Federal skirmishers were sent out, Sergeant Henry F. Weaver, of Company C, Sixth U.S. Heavy Artillery (colored) reported the following: "We were ordered to take possession of two 10 ponder Parrott guns (these guns were in position just outside the fort), and soon another order to take them inside the works, which

Colonel A.A. Russell
(photo taken after the war)

was done immediately and put in battery on the south end of the works. Lieutenant McClure taking command of the right gun and giving me the left gun, for which I had to build a platform before it could be used to any effect; but the platform was built and the gun in position, and I was firing at the advancing enemy as they came in sight. In the mean-time Company B, Thirteenth Tennessee Cavalry, had left their camp on a hill in front of our main fort and came rushing back in disorder, leaving their horses and all their camp equipment behind. The rebels soon commenced running off the horses under brisk fire of musketry and a selection of artillery of Company D, Second U.S. Light Artillery (colored), commanded by First Lieutenant Hunter, still farther to the left was a selection of light artillery, manned by Company A, Sixth U.S. Heavy Artillery, under the command of Captain Epenter and Lieutenant Bishoff.

Booth and Bradford did not attempt to hold the outer line, but trained their artillery so as to play upon the only roads leading through it. The fight was opened at daylight by Confederate Colonel McCulloch. He moved cautiously through the ravines and short hills which incompass the place, protecting the men as much as possible from the enemy's artillery, five pieces of which the fort, aided by two gun-boats on the river, played furiously upon him. Moving in this manner he succeeded about 11 o' clock in taking the work, which I have spoken of as been commenced by General Villepigue, and the flag of the eighteenth Mississippi battalion, Lieutenant-Colonel Chalmers commanding, which had been the first regiment to enter the fort, was quickly flying above it.

Lieutenant Hill, Company C, Sixth U.S. and post Adjutant, was killed while outside the fort setting fire to the quarters of the Thirteenth Cavalry, his intention was to burn the small cabins down, and prevent the rebel sharpshooters from gaining access to them and directing a deadly fire upon the fort's inhabitants. Not long after Hill was

Presently existing slough where the Mississippi River was located during the Fort Pillow Battle (Mississippi River changed its course one mile to the West due to a slide in 1902). It was here That Captain Marshall from the Union Gunboat "New Era" had been firing into the Confederates during the battle. This photo was made south of Fort Pillow and the fort cannot be seen in this photo, it is located just outside of the picture to the right side of the photo.

killed, Major Booth was struck in the chest and mortally wounded. Hardy N. Revelle, a dry goods clerk at Fort Pillow who chose to stay and help defend the fort, witnessed the death of Major Booth: "I was standing not more than 10 paces from Major Booth when he fell, struck in the heart by a musket-bullet. It was but a few minutes past 9. He did not die immediately, but was borne from the field.

Mean while Confederate Colonel McCulloch had been moving up on the left, Colonel Bell moved up on the right and rear, and colonel Wilson moved up on the center, taking advantage of the ravines as much as possible to shelter their men.

Affairs were in this condition, with the main fort completely invested, when Major-General Forrest arrived with Colonel Wisdom's regiment of Bufords division. Forrest's

Photo of first line taken by McCulloch and location of Forrest's headquarters during the remainder of the battle.

McCulloch taking first line, as the outnumbered Federal Cavalry scramble to the safety of the main fort.

Confederate Sharpshooters picking off Federal Soldiers inside Fort Pillow.

official report states that he arrived at the scene at 10 a.m. upon his arrival Forrest rode in the open to view the fort and surrounding ravines, while doing so he had two horses shot out from under him, one horse died so frantically that it fell onto Forrest and bruised him badly, acting Adjutant General Charles W. Anderson pleaded with Forrest to dismount before he gets himself shot, Forrest replied no, that he was just as apt to be hit one way as another, and he could see better on horseback.

Forrest ordered General Chalmers to advance his lines and gain position on the slope, where our men would be perfectly protected from the heavy fire of artillery and musketry, as the enemy could not depress their pieces so as to rake the slopes, nor could they fire on them with small-arms except by mounting the breast-works and exposing themselves to the fire of our sharpshooters, who, under cover of stumps and logs, forced them to keep down inside the works.

About noon the rebels soon advanced close up to the fort, getting into the houses of the cavalry that Federal Lieutenant Hill had given his life trying to destroy and prevent access to the rebels. The rebels also gained possession of some rifle-pits the Federals had made just a few days earlier, which proved more use to them than it did the Federals, The rebels kept up such a brisk fire that it was almost impossible for the Federals to work the cannons. The cannoneers were all killed or wounded with exception of one or two, also Lieutenant Hunter's gun and Sergeant Weaver's gun were almost out of ammunition. Weaver states that not more than one out of five shells burst, owing to poor fuses.

After several hours hard fighting Forrest had gained the desired position, not however, without considerable loss. Our main line was now within an average distance of 100 yards from the fort, and extended from Coal creek, on the right, to the bluff, or bank, of the Mississippi river on the left. Forrest's offical report states that his main line was within 100 yards of the fort at the time he sent a demand for surrender, General Chalmers offical report states that they took possesion of all the rifle-pits around the fort, and closed up on all sides within 25 or 30 yards of the outer ditch before a surrender was sent in.

During the entire mourning the gun-boat kept a continued fire in all directions, but without effect, and Forrest being confident in his ability to take the fort by assualt, and desiring to prevent further loss of life, sent with a Captain W.A. Goodman, under a flag of truce, the following demand for unconditional surrender of the garrison.

Headquarters, Forrest's Cavalry,
Before Fort Pillow, April 12, 1864
Major Booth, Commanding United States Forces, Fort Pillow:
   Major,—— The conduct of the officers and men garrisoning Fort Pillow has been such as to entitle them to being treated as prisoners of war. I demand the unconditional surrender of this garrison, promising you that you all shall be treated as prisoners of war. My men have received a fresh supply of ammunition, and from their present position can easily assualt and capture the fort. Should my demand be refused, I cannot be responsible for the fate of your command.
respectfully,
N.B. Forrest,
Major-General Commanding

   Major Bradford had taken over command of the fort after Major Booth had been killed. Bradford thought it better to keep the knowledge of Booth's death a secret from Forrest, he forged Booth's signature on his reply, and answered him as if Booth were still alive. Bradford's forged reply requested that he be given one hour to consult with his officers and the gun-boat "New Era", standing off shore.
   The gun-boat "New Era', had ceased firing during the flag of truce, but the smoke of three other boats ascending the river was in plain view to Forrest and his men, the foremost boat the "Olive Branch", was crowded with Federal troops, Forrest believed the request for an hour was Booths' attempt to gain time for re-enforcements to arrive. Forrest then replied in writing that he only demanded the surrender of the fort and not of the gun-boat and would only allow Booth twenty minutes for a decision, Forrest orderd Captain Goodman to remain at the truce sight for a final answer.
   During this time Bradfords brother Theodorick was communicating by signal flag with Captain Marshall of the gun-boat New Era, Marshall had agreed to rake the fort with canister [A cannon load that had the effect of a giant shot gun] as the Confederates entered the fort and after the Federals had taken refuge below the bluff. At the same time Captain Marshall had also agreed to make arraingements to pick up all the Federal soldiers at the waters edge and remove them to safety. With this knowledge in hand, Major Bradford and all the other officers agreed not to surrender the fort and become prisoners, they would gambel on Captain Marshall's ability to succur them from this untenable posistion which they found themselves in.
   After some delay, and seeing a message delivered to Captain Goodman, Forrest rode up himself to were the notes were received and delivered. Bradfords answer to Forrest was handed him, written in pencil on a slip of paper, without envelope, and as well as Forrest could later remember it was as follows: "Negotiations will not attain the desired object." As the officers who were in charge of the Federal flag of truce had expressed a doubt as to Forrest's presence, and had pronounced the demand a trick, He handed them back a note saying: "I am General Forrest; go back and say to major Booth that I demand an answer in plain, unmistakable English. Will he fight or surrender?" Returning to his original posistion, before the expiration of twenty minutes he

received the following reply: "General: I will not surrender. Very respectfully, your obediant servant, L.F. Booth, commanding U.S. Forces, Fort Pillow."

While these negotiations were pending the steamers from below were rapidly approaching the fort. The foremost was the ***Olive Branch***, whose position and movements indicated to Forrest that she intended to land. A few shots fired into her caused her to leave the shore and make for the opposite side of the river. One other boat possibly the ***Glendale*** passed up on the far side of the river, the third one turned back. During the truce John F. Ray of Company B, Thirteenth Tennessee Cavalry testified that the Confederates were massing and disposing their forces while the flag was under consideration. He also states that at this time he saw some rebels come even to the ditch beyond which the forts cannon were placed.

They were close enough that he could ask them why they came in so close while the flag of truce was being canvassed. They only replied that they knew their business there. When they jumped into the ditch outside the fort, Ray and others threatened to fire on them if they came any nearer.

The twenty minutes having expired, Forrest directed Brigadier-General Chalmers to prepare for the asault. Bell's brigade occupied the right, with his extreme right resting on Coal Creek. McCulloch's brigade occupied the left, extending from the center of the river. Three companies of McCulloch's regiment were placed in an old rifle-pit

Major Bradford's reply being given to General Forrest by Lt. Leaming.

on the left and almost to the rear of the fort, which had evidently been thrown up for protection of sharpshooters or riflemen in supporting the water batteries below. On the right a portion of Barteu's regiment, of Bell's brigade, was also under the bluff and in the rear of the fort.

Forrest dispatched staff officers to Colonel Bell and McCulloch, commanding brigades, to say to them that Forrest would watch with interest the conduct of the troops; that Missourians, Mississippians, and Tennesseeans surrounded the works, and that he desired to see which would first scale the fort. Fearing gun-boats and transports might attempt a landing, Forrest directed his aide-de-camp, Captain Charles W. Anderson, to assume command of the three companies on the left and rear of the fort and hold the position against anything that might come by land or water, but to take no part in the assualt on the fort.

Everything being ready, the bugle sounded the charge, which was made with a Rebel Yell.

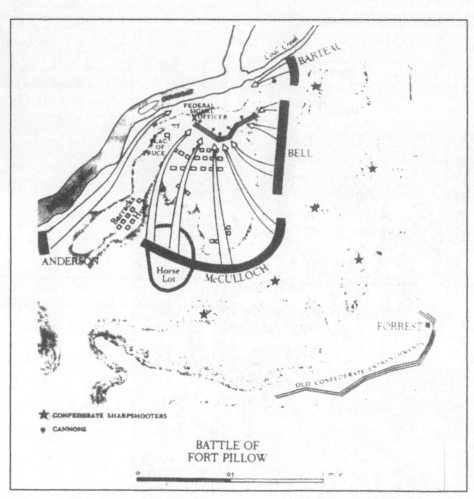

★ CONFEDERATE SHARPSHOOTERS
● CANNONS

BATTLE OF
FORT PILLOW

Federal soldiers retreating towards the bluff as Confederates fire into the fort from the top of the fort wall.

Dry Goods Clerk Hardy N. Revelle who was helping defend the fort against Forrest states: "It was about 2:30 in the afternoon that a large force of infantry came upon them from the ravine toward the east of where I stood. It seemed to come down Coal Creek. They charged upon our ranks. Another large force of rebel Cavalry charged from the south of east, and another force from the north. They mounted the breast-works at the first charge where I stood. We fired upon them while upon the breast-works. I remember firing two shots while the enemy were upon the walls." Confederate Lieutenant-Colonel Reed, temporarily commanding the Fifth Mississippi Cavalry, was pre-eminently daring, and fell mortally wounded while standing on the rifle-pits and encouraging his men to charge, and Lieutenant Burton was killed at his side.

Both black and white, fought manfully. Several negroes wounded, with blood running from their bodies, were still engaged loading and firing cannon and muskets cheerfully.

The negro troops, after realizing they could no longer resist, and fearing as thay had been told by their officers, that Forrest would kill them if they surrenderd, made a break and ran down the bluff, surrendering their arms as the rebels came down the fortification.

When the white men found that there was no quarter to be shown, and that (white and black) were to be butchered. They also gave up their arms and passed down the bluff, they were followed closely and fiercely by the advancing rebel forces, their fire never ceasing at all."

Captain Theodorick Bradford, Major Bradfords brother who with a blue signal flag had been signaling the gun-boat **New Era** was noticed by General Forrest who had entered the fort after the garrison had retreated down the bluff, Forrest was heard to say, "shoot that man with the black flag." This was after the Federal flag had been hauled down and the fort surrenderd. Federal witnesses said Captain Bradfords body was literally shot to pieces by numerous Confederate soldiers.

Confederate Sergeant Achilles V. Clark of the Twentieth Tennessee would write his sister a week later. "The poor deluded Negroes would run up to our men fall on their knees and with uplifted hands scream for mercy but were ordered to their feet and then shot down. The white men fared but little better. Their Fort turned out to be a great slaughter pen. Blood, human blood stood about in pools and brains could have been gathered up in any quanity. I with several others tried to stop the butchery and at one time had partially succeeded but General Forrest oredered them shot down like dogs, and the carnage continued.

As the Federals descended the bluff an enfilading and deadly fire was poured into them by the troops under Captain Anderson, on the left, and Barteu's detachment on the right.

Until this fire was opened upon them, at a distance varying from 30 to 100 yards, they were evidently ignorant of any force having gained their rear. The regiment who had stormed the fort from above also poured a destructive fire into the rear and down the bluff on top of the retreating and now panick-stricken and almost decimated garrison.

Once the Federals had reached the bottom of the bluff, and realized that the gunboat New Era had closed its portals and was steaming upstream away from the fort, they panicked, many ran southward into the posistion of Major Anderson's men, Anderson states: "When driven from the works, the garrison retreated towards the river, with guns in hand, and firing back, and as soon as in view we opened fire on them, and continued it rapidly until the Federal flag came down, Colonel Barteau held the posistion below the bluff on the northern end of the garrison opposite Anderson's posistion, when the Federals found no means of escape from Anderson's posistion they retreated towards Barteau's posistion, in his affidavit he states that a number of Federals, after others had surrendered, continued to fight beneath the bluff until they were shot down. "They were in a frenzy of excitement or drunken delirium. Some even, who had thrown down their arms, took them up again and continued firing. Some of my own men had to take down the flag [Private John Doak Carr, who died in 1897, at Hartsville, Tennessee.] The Federals did not do it, nor at any time make a surrender.

General Chalmers states: "Some of the Federals, mostly negroes, who in fright or despiration broke through the Confederates in the effort to escape, were pursued and shot, as were those who attempted escape by swimming down the river. Some of these were killed and some few succeded in getting away.

Anderson states: "To the best of my knowledge and belief it did not exceed twenty minutes from the time our bugles sounded for the assualt until the fort was in our possesion and firing had ceased on every part of the ground. Anderson further stated that he believed that the heavy loss in killed and wounded during the retreat was alone due to the incapacity of their commander, the drunken condition of the men, and the fatal agreement with and promise of Captain Marshall of the New Era to protect and succor them when driven from the works.

Mack J. Leaming, Lieutenant and Adjutant of the Thirteenth Tennessee Cavalry (U.S.) reported: "After the Sixth U.S.

Major Charles W. Anderson

Artillary rushed down the bluff, the Thirteenth Cavalry threw down their arms and surrenderd. For a moment the fire seemed to slacken. The scene which followed, however, beggars all description. The enemy carried our works at about 4 p.m., and from that time on until dark, and at intervals throughout the night, our men were shot down without mercy and almost without regard to color. This horrid work of butchery did not cease even with the night of murder, but was renewed again the next morning. When numbers of our wounded were basely murdered after a long night of pain and suffering on the field where they had fought so bravely."

General Bell testified: After the Federal flag had been hauled down "The captured prisoners were then detailed to bury their dead. Between sunset and dark we moved out with our command and the prisoners, and camped about fifteen miles back in the country. The statements in relation to alledged 'cruelty and barbarism' practiced by Forrest's command are a tissue of lies from end to end.

Adjutant Mack Leaming reported that the rebels were very bitter against the loyal tennesseans, terming them "home made Yankees," and declaring they would give them no better treatment than they dealt out to Negro troops with whom they were fighting.

Leaming goes on to report that at about 10 a.m. the day following the capture of the fort, while the U.S. gun-boat no. 28 from Memphis was shelling the enemy, who at the same time was engaged in murdering our wounded, Forrest sent a flag of truce to the commander granting him from that time until 5 p.m. to bury our dead and remove the few surviving wounded, he having no means of attending to them. This proposal was accepted, and under it myself with some 59 others, all that were left of the wounded,

Photo of ditch outside south end of fort wall, it was here that all the dead Federal soldiers were buried in a mass grave. After the war the bodies were exumed, marked, and transported to Memphis for re-burial. While in transit the names marked on the wood coffins with charcoal were washed away in a rain storm leaving most of those men as un-knowns.

were carried on board the transport **Platte Valley** and taken to Mound City, Ill., where we received good care and treatment in the U.S. General Hospital at that place.

Leaming also states: "The bravery of our troops in the defense of Fort Pillow, I think, cannot be questioned. Many of the men, and particularly the colored soldiers, had never before been under fire; yet every man did his duty with a courage and determined resolution, seldom if ever surpassed in similar engagements.

In a report by Forrest, he states: The approximate Federal loss was upward of 500 killed, but few of the officers escaping. Forrest goes on to say, "It is hoped that these facts will demonstrate to the Northern people that negro soldiers cannot cope with Southerners."

South end of main fort where Theodorick Bradford was posistioned during his signaling to the Gun boat "New Era". The surrender terms were made to the right of this photograph outside the fort walls. The bluff is to the left of this photograph. Bell's Brigade entered the fort from the location of the cannon in this photo and left to the North end in the upper left corner of this photo. McCulloch enetered from the right side of the cannon all the way to the photographers location. Forrest entered the Fort at the far laft corner of the fort in this photo (North end).

Photo taken at the bottom of the bluff where the majority of Federal soldiers were killed.

The North end of the fort, it was at this location that General Forrest entered the fort. The bluff is on the right side of this photo behind the tree line, the Federal soldiers tried to escape down the bluff to the waters edge as the Confederates came over the walls.

FORT PILLOW CASUALTY INFORMATION AND PERSONAL INFORMATION ON THE MEMBERS OF THE 13TH TN CAVALRY CO. A

(BRADFORD'S BATTALION)

NAME	ENLIST.	MUSTER	AGE	RANK	AFTER BATTLE
John Gregory	10/26/1863		24	1 LT	No record
George Craig	8/19/1863		28	1 Ser	No record
James B Phipps	9/04/1863		44	QMS	Captured
William R Fornshee	10/10/1863		18	CSS	No record
Randolph C Gunter	11/20/1863		1	DS	Captured
Steph W Sutterfield	10/06/1863		26	2 S	No record
Thomas F Burton	8/18/1863		32	3 S	Captured/Died in prison Andersonville/July/14/1864
Nathen C Wiggs	9/16/1863			4 S	No record
Valentia V Methany	11/09/1863		18	5 S	Captured/Died in prison Andersonville
William R Albritton	8/18/1863		24	COR	MIA/Probably killed
Henry H Williams	8/22/1863		23	COR	Admitted to Paducah Hosp. in April, died in May, cause of death not given
David M Burton	8/26/1863		21	COR	Captured/Died in prison Andersonville/October/11/1864
Andrew J Glass	11/30/1863			COR	Killed
Elijah F Burcham	10/10/1863		24	COR	Killed
John W Babb	8/18/1863		21	COR	No record
Thomas J Morgan	9/06/1863		18	COR	No record
William H Martin	11/22/1863			COR	No record
Rial D Allen	9/19/1863		45	BKSM	No record
Ephraim L Churchwell	11/19/1863		27	BKSM	Captured/Died in prison Andersonville
Thomas J Powell	11/22/1863			WGNR	No record
Charles Anderson	10/02/1863		35	Privt	No record
Francis Anderson	10/20/1863		31	Privt	Status uncertain/maybe not there/released from confinement
EzekielArnold	8/24/1863		33	Privt	No record
WilliamAlbritton	8/18/1863		24	Privt	Survived wounds
WilliamAdkinson	11/01/1863			Privt	No record
RichardAAdkinson	11/01/1863			Privt	No record
PeterAntoine	11/23/1863			Privt	Captured/Died in prison Andersonville

George W Burcham	11/01/1863	21	Privt	Killed (George A Burcham)
JamesDBurcham	12/01/1863		Privt	Norecord
Chris C Burcham	11/30/1863		Privt	No record
JohnBurcham	11/30/1863		Privt	No record
Robert W Blelock	11/08/1863	41	Privt	Killed (Robert W Blalock)
WilliamBohanon	11/01/1863	30	Privt	No record
Issac Beckner	12/01/1863		Privt	No record
George W Babb	11/25/1863		Privt	Captured/Died in prison Andersonville
Thos J Cartwright	9/26/1863	17	Privt	Survived wounds
Woodford H ooksey	10/02/1863	42	Privt	Died of wounds
Jas M Christenburg	9/24/1863	30	Privt	Captured/Survived prison (James M Christenburg)
William F Carter	9/24/1863	31	Privt	Killed
JamesClark	9/24/1863	43	Privt	Captured/Died in prison Andersonville
CarrolCallison	11/01/1863	19	Privt	MIA/probably killed Widow filed pension papers
James C Childer	11/24/1863		Privt	Captured/Died in prison Andersonville
GeorgeH Dunn	11/20/1863		Privt	No record
Daniel Etter	12/01/1863		Privt	No record
William Frazier	12/01/1863		Privt	No record
Josiah M Forrester	8/18/1863	18	Privt	Status uncertain/maybe not there/present in Jan/Feb
Pitcher HGregory	10/16/1863	18	Privt	No record
Lynn B Gregory	9/08/1863	20	Privt	No record
Amos L Gaskins	8/24/1863	24	Privt	No record
William Goodrich	8/19/1863		Privt	No record
John L Gooden	11/25/1863		Privt	Status uncertain/maybe not there/present in Jan/Feb
Joseph M Green Hospital Register	12/01/1863		Privt	Survived wounds/Mound City
Thomas M Hardison	10.05.1863	19	Privt	Paroled sick/Memphis Hosp. Register
Preston Hankins	9/16/1863	32	Privt	Norecord
Richard Heathcot	8/24/1863	26	Privt	Died of wounds/reference in St. Louis Democrat Paper/April 16th 1864
Jackson T Hanwell	11/10/1863	24	Privt	Captured
Garrett Hanes	11/22/1863		Privt	Captured/Died in prison Andersonville
John Halford	11/30/1863		Privt	No record
Joseph Halford	12/01/1863		Privt	Captured/Died in prison Andersonville
Joseph James	10/02/1863	18	Privt	Norecord
Andrew J Knight	11/20/1863		Privt	Captured
George W Kirk	12/01/1863		Privt	Captured
MichealL ydon	8/18/1863	27	Privt	No record
John W Long	9/05/1863	21	Privt	Captured/died in prison Andersonville
William F Lovett	11/09/1863	18	Privt	Captured/Died in prison Andersonville (William T Lovett)
Thomas Loftis	11/02/1863		Privt	Survived wounds/Memphis Hospital Register

Name	Date	Age	Rank	Notes
John E Lemmons	11/23/1863		Privt	Captured/Died in prison Andersonville
James H. Lindsley	11/30/1863		Privt	No record
Charles W Mekel	10/02/1863	28	Privt	No record
James P Michenor	9/24/1863	18	Privt	Status uncertain/maybe not there/present in Jan/Feb
Benjamin F Miller	9/04/1863	27	Privt	No record
Mark McKenzie	9/04/1863	18	Privt	Killed
James W Mingeor	8/31/1863	18	Privt	Captured/Died in prison Andersonville
James P Meador	9/24/1863	18	Privt	Survived wounds
Marcus Mitchum	11/03/1863		Privt	Captured/Died in prison Andersonville
James Moore	11/20/1863		Privt	Captured/Died in prison Andersonville
James W Mitchell	11/08/1863	21	Privt	Jones M Mitchell MIA William L Mitchell died of wounds/otherwise no record
Sandy Mathews	11/28/1863		Privt	No record
William McDonald	10/19/1863	26	Privt	No record
Robert W Nelson	8/19/1863	22	Privt	No record
Jasper Nipper	8/19/1863	17	Privt	Captured
James Nelson	11/23/1863		Privt	Paroled sick/Memphis Hospital Register
William Norcutt	11/30/1863		Privt	No record
James W Nealy	8/18/1863	29	Privt	No record
Calvin M Prince	9/13/1863		Privt	Survived wounds/Memphis Hospital Register
Sylvester B Paul	11/08/1863	19	Privt	No record
James Park	11/24/1863		Privt	Died of wounds
Wiley Robinson	11/19/1863	18	Privt	Died of wounds
George Riggs	11/26/1863		Privt	MIA/Present in Jan/Feb
John C Simmons	8/18/1863	25	Privt	Survived wounds Discharged as 6th Tn Cav Possibly captured
Samuel S Stafford	8/24/1863		Privt	No record
Carroll Sweeney	8/24/1863	32	Privt	Captured/Survived
David Sneed	11/24/1863		Privt	Survived wounds
Archie F Taylor	11/01/1863		Privt	No record
John B Tatum	11/28/1863		Privt	No record
William C Talor	8/26/1863	18	Privt	No record
John C Williams	9/23/1863	25	Privt	No record
Samuel E Wilkins	9/26/1863	20	Privt	No record
Henry I Wilkins	11/09/1863	19	Privt	No record
Charles J Wallace	11/01/1863		Privt	No record
Addison H White	11/30/1863		Privt	Status uncertain Present as of Jan 29th

Fort Pillow Casualty Information And Personal Information On The Members Of The U.S. 6th Heavy Artillary, Colored.

Name	Status	Name	Status
Jessie Addison	Survived wounds	Joseph Alexander	Killed
Sandy Addison	Escaped	Elijah Allfond	Killed
Thomas Addison	Survived wounds	James Allen	Killed
Ransom Anderson	Survived wounds	Joseph Allen	Killed

John Archy	Killed	Charles Fox	Killed
Isaac Atman	Killed	Thomas Gaddis	Died from wounds
Harvey Atwood	Killed	Joseph Gallin	Killed
Samual Bailey	Killed	Dorsey Garret	Survived wounds
William Bell	Killed	Harrison Garl	Killed
Peter Bishoff	Captured	Peter Garner	Killed
Edward Biggers	Escaped	William Gaylord	Survived wounds
Cyrus Blackmun	Killed	John Gentry	Captured ***
Dudley Bland	Killed	Dennis Gibbs	Killed
Adam Bond	Escaped	Henry Gibson	Killed
Lionel F. Booth Major	Killed	Hampton Gilchrist	Escaped
Aaron Bowers	Killed	Richard Glover	Killed
Nelson Box	Killed	Willis Granbury	Killed
Joseph Boyd	Escaped	Harrison Green	Killed
James Bridges	Killed	Robert Green	Killed
Jackson Brown	Killed	Benjamin Green	Killed
Ralph Brunson	Killed	Samuel Green	Captured
Armstead Burgess	Captured	Thomas Green	Captured
Hurnton Burnett	Killed	Peter Grey	Killed
Hardin Caison	Survived wounds	Isaac Griffin	Captured
Edward Caldwell	Killed	Handy Gwin	Killed
John Campbell	Killed	Robert Hall	Died from wounds
Adam Carpenter	Escaped	Henry Hanks	Survived wounds
Delos Carson	Killed	Perry Hardaway	Captured
Henry Christian	Survived wounds	Duncan Harden	Survived wounds
Solomon Chuson	Killed	Fayette Hardin	Killed
Sandy Cole	Survived wounds	Reeses Hardin	Killed
James Collier	Killed	Braxton Harris	Escaped
Alford Coleman	Escaped	Carol Harris	Escaped
Eli Cothel	Survived wounds	Jackson Harris	Killed
Washington Cox	Killed	Aaron Harrison	Killed
Jesse Crocks	Killed	A.G. Hatfield	Captured ***
Charles Cross	Killed	James Hayes	Killed
Washington Daniels	Killed	James Henderson	Captured
Alexander Davey	Killed	John Hennesy	Captured
Thomas Davis	Killed	Samuel Hueston	Killed
Benton Deloni	Killed	Henry Hill	Captured ***
Richard Dickens	Killed	John Hill	Killed
Henry Dix	Captured	Samuel Hill	Killed
Jeff Dobbs	Captured	Matthew Hilton	Killed
Robert Dotson	Died from wounds	Frank Hogan	Escaped
Elijah Dorsey	Killed	John Hogan	Captured
Robert Duncan	Killed	Robert Hogan	Killed
Arthus Edmonds	Survived wounds	Thomas Hooper	Killed
Frederick Edmonds	Killed	Alexander Howard	Killed
William Ellis	Escaped	Albert Hudson	Killed
Charles Epenter	Captured	Alec Hunter	Killed
Elias Falls	Died from wounds	Nathen Hunter	Survived wounds
Aaron Fenders	Survived wounds	George Huston	Escaped
Albert Flate	Survived wounds #	Elias Irving	Captured
Green Fleeming	Killed	Gideon Irwin	Killed
Joseph Fleming	Killed	Wesley Irwin	Escaped
Marion Fleming	Killed	Willis Ivory	Captured
James Fort	Died from wounds	Charles Jackson	Killed
Joseph Foster	Killed	Josephus Jackson	Killed

Allen James	Captured
Melville Jenks	Captured
Joseph Jobber	Killed
Nelson Johnson	Killed
Rayford Johnson	Killed
Wilson Johnson	Captured
Washington Joliff	Killed
Benjamin Jones	Survived wounds
Hartwell Jones	Killed
Henry Jones	Killed
Nathaniel Jones	Killed
Reuben Jones	Killed
Joseph Key	Killed
Charles Keye	Survived wounds
John Keys	Killed
Parker King	Killed
Daniel Lacey	Escaped
David Laird	Captured
Henry Lane	Killed
Anderson Lee	Escaped
Willis Leggett	Escaped
David Lester	Killed
James Lewis	Survived wounds
William Lincoln	Killed
Henry Lippett	Died from wounds
Green Lott	Killed
Charles Mackley	Killed
Robert Macks	Killed
Henry Martin	Killed
Peter Martin	Killed
William May	Killed
Thomas McClure	Captured
Wesley McDowell	Killed
Lewis McGee	Killed
James McKenny	Captured
Frank Meeks	Killed
Marshall Mercer	Killed
Ronald Mercer	Killed
Phillip Michem	Escaped
Adam Middleton	Killed
Essick Middleton	Killed
Simon Middleton	Killed
John Miles	Escaped
London Mooney	Killed
Thomas Morgan	Killed
William Morgan	Killed
William Morris	Escaped
Nathen Motley	Died from wounds
Charles Mullins	Killed
Fleming Mullins	Killed
William Mullins	Captured
George Murrill	Killed
Houston Murrill	Captured
James Murrill	Captured
Alexander Naison	Survived wounds
Benjamin Jones	Survived wounds
Hartwell Jones	Killed
Henry Jones	Killed
Nathaniel Jones	Killed
Reuben Jones	Killed
Joseph Key	Killed
Charles Keye	Survived wounds
John Keys	Killed
Parker King	Killed
Daniel Lacey	Escaped
David Laird	Captured
Henry Lane	Killed
Anderson Lee	Escaped
Willis Leggett	Escaped
David Lester	Killed
James Lewis	Survived wounds
William Lincoln	Killed
Henry Lippett	Died from wounds
Green Lott	Killed
Charles Mackley	Killed
Robert Macks	Killed
Henry Martin	Killed
Peter Martin	Killed
William May	Killed
Thomas McClure	Captured
Wesley McDowell	Killed
Lewis McGee	Killed
James McKenny	Captured
Frank Meeks	Killed
Marshall Mercer	Killed
Ronald Mercer	Killed
Phillip Michem	Escaped
Adam Middleton	Killed
Essick Middleton	Killed
Simon Middleton	Killed
John Miles	Escaped
London Mooney	Killed
Thomas Morgan	Killed
William Morgan	Killed
William Morris	Escaped
Nathen Motley	Died from wounds
Charles Mullins	Killed
Fleming Mullins	Killed
William Mullins	Captured
George Murrill	Killed
Houston Murrill	Captured
James Murrill	Captured
Alexander Naison	Survived wounds
Emanuel Nichols	Survived wounds
Thomas Norris	Killed
William Oates	Escaped
Walter Ogilles	Captured
Nelson Paden	Captured
John Padon	Killed
Henry Parker	Survived wounds

Name	Status	Name	Status
Cyrus Paschall	Survived wounds	James Taylor	Killed
William Paton	Killed	Robert Taylor	Killed
Solomon Patrick	Captured	Thomas Taylor	Killed
Henry Patty	Died from wounds *	William Taylor	Killed
Coleman Payne	Killed	William H. Taylor	Killed
Albert Pearson	Killed	John Thompson	Captured
Thomas Piggie	Killed	Ed Trice	Captured ***
Burrill Pope	Captured	Roach Turner	Escaped
Coolie Pride	Died from wounds	Jerry Tyson	Killed
James Pride	Captured ***	Henry Underwood	Killed
John Pritchard	Killed	Henderson Van	Killed
Joseph Pritchard	Escaped	Daniel Vanhorn	Survived wounds ##
Allen Pyle	Killed	George Wade	Killed
Samuel Raban	Killed	Nelson Wadford	Killed
Donald Ray	Killed	John Wadford	Killed
James Ricks	Killed	William Wallace	Killed
Marcellus Robertson	Killed	Cornelius Waller	Killed
Benjamin Robinson	Survived wounds	Green Waltz	Killed
Benjamin Robinson	Killed	William Ward	Captured
Joseph Robinson	Died from wounds **	Jospeh Warren	Killed
Berry Rogers	Killed	George Washington	Captured
Elwin Rollins	Killed	Claiburne Watson	Killed
Andy Ryan	Killed	Julius Watson	Killed
Oliver Scott	Killed	Henry F. Weaver	Escaped ##
Sandy Scruggs	Killed	Isaac Weaver	Killed
Frank Shakleford	Killed	Samuel Webster	Killed
George Shaw	Survived wounds #	George Wilbury	Killed
Sandy Sherman	Killed	Charles Williams	Captured
Pompey Simmons	Killed	Henry Williams	Killed
Andy Simmons	Killed	Peter Williams	Captured
Henry Simmons	Killed	Thomas Williams	Killed
Lewis Simpson	Killed	Jacob Wilson	Escaped
Fate Sledge	Escaped	Boston Winston	Killed
Judge Sledge	Killed	James Winston	Captured
John Smith	Killed	Robert Winston	Killed
William Smith	Killed	Henry Wood	Killed
Jacob Southard	Killed	Henry Worr	Killed
Jerry Stewart	Escaped	Joseph Young	Killed
Joshua Stevens	Killed	Phillip Young	Escaped
William Stitt	Killed	William Young	Killed
Jim Stokes	Escaped		
Joseph Strong	Captured		
Nathen Stubbs	Killed		
Samuel Summerhill	Killed		
Samuel Tangsley	Killed		
Moses Tansal	Killed		
Henry Tarlton	Killed		
Henry Tate	Killed		
Ellis Taylor	Escaped		
Henry Taylor	Killed		

Congressional report list him at Mound City Hospital (CSR just says he died).

** *Regimental return of May 10th (CSR just says he died).*

*** *Jordan & Pryor POW list.*

Mound City Hospital Register.

OR, Ser. 1, XXXIII, pt. 1, 510 (vanhorn), 538-539 (Weaver)

FROM FORT PILLOW TO ANDERSONVILLE PRISON

W.R. Mclagan, a citizen of the United States, being first duly sworn, states upon oath that for the last two years he has been trading between Saint Louis, Mo., and Covington, Tenn.; that at the time of the attack upon Fort Pillow, April 12th, 1864, he was at Covington, Tenn., and was taken by General Forrest as a conscript on the 13th of April, with about 30 other citizens; that on the evening of the 12th of April Major Bradford, Thirteenth Tennessee Cavalry, U.S. forces arrived at Covington under guard as prisoners of war, and was reported as such to Colonel Duckworth, commanding Seventh Tennessee Cavalry, Confederate forces; that on the 13th of April Major Bradford and conscripts, including the affiant, were placed in charge of two companies of the Seventh Tennessee Cavalry, Captain Russell and Lawler commanding. They were taken to Brownsville, Tenn., and started from there to Jackson, Tenn.

When they had proceeded about 5 miles from Brownsville a halt was made, and Major Bradford was taken about 50 yards from the command by guard of 5 Confederate soldiers in charge of a Lieutenant, and was there deliberately shot, 3 of the Confederate soldiers discharging their fire-arms, all of which took effect, killing him instantly. This was on the 14th day of April, 1864, near dusk; that the body of Major Bradford was left unburied in the woods about 50 yards from the road.

The affiant, with the other conscripts, was taken on to Jackson, and on the 22nd day of April the affiant and 25 others of the conscripts made their escape from the Confederate forces at Jackson. On the way back he saw the body of Major Bradford lying in the same place where he was shot. This was on Saturday night, the 23d of April. Major Bradford, before he was shot, fell on his knees and said that he had fought them manfully, and wished to be treated as a prisoner of war.

The only Officers to survive the Battle were Adjutant Leaming, Lieutenant Porter and Lieutenant Logan, Porter and Logan soon died in a Confederate Prison for officers in Macon Georgia.

Since Memphis and Corinth were occupied by Federal troops, Thomas and the other prisoners were marched to Jackson Tennessee, they left Jackson on board a train which took them to Holly Springs Mississippi, while at Holly Springs, Phillip Young, a prisoner from Company A, Sixth Heavy Artillery (colored), stated that there were 104 white men prisoners and about 30 colored men prisoners. The prisoners were marched from holly Springs to Ripley Mississippi.

A diary written by Union soldier, Third Sergeant James H. Dennison, of Company K, 113th Illinois Infantry, gives a day by day account of his life in the army and his capture by Nathan Forrest at the battle of Brice's Cross roads located east of Ripley

Photo of James H. Dennison

Mississippi. he gives a detailed description of the route to Andersonville Prison and the hardships he suffered along the way. Thomas Burton, his brother David and others traveled this same route and would have seen and experienced similar hardships.

June 12th 1864:

Ripley Mississippi, We are in the court house, there is about one hundred of us, it is a very dirty place. I have had nothing to eat but what I have begged from them that had some.

June 13th:

Left Ripley at 5 0'clock last night and marched four miles, camped, started at 8 o'clock marched all day, got to railroad at seven.

June 14th:

Got aboard the cars (train) last night at eight o'clock at Guntown Mississippi, we drawed rations, this is the Mobile and Charlston railroad, a fine country, I feel well.

June 15th:

We are at Meridian Mississippi, we got off train here to rest, we stayed all day and night, there was one man shot, we got corn bread.

June 16th:

Left Meridian at 5 o'clock on the cars, run all day, got to Selma Alabama and got aboard a boat on the Alabama River, running up the river.

June 17th:

We are going up river very slow, we have not had any rations today. The boys had parch corn, we are awful dirty, we got to Montgomery Alabama.

Note:

At about this time some of the colored prisoners were taken to Mobile, Alabama, the following correspondence was found in the Official Records:

Mobile, May 20, 1864.

General COOPER, Adjutant and Inspector General:

Some Negroes captured by General Forrest at Fort Pillow sent here. Put them to work on fortifications. Chief engineers will keep records of the time in order to remunerate their owners. Is my action approved?

DABNEY H. MAURY,

Major-General, Commanding.

Richmond, Va., May 21, 1864.

General D.H. MAURY, Mobile, Ala.:

Your employment of the Negroes captured by General Forrest is approved.

S. COOPER,

Adjutant and Inspector General.

June 18th: Montgomery, Alabama.

This is quite a big place, we have got rations this morning, feel well, we are aboard the cars, run all day, rained, got to Columbus Georgey, stayed in the streets all night.

June 19th:

Left Columbus at 4 o'clock, run all day, we was on open cars, rained all day, Andersonville Military Prison at 4 o'clock, a hard place.

June 20th:

Andersonville Georgey, rained all afternoon, laid out on the wet ground, did not get any corn bread, this is a crowded place, I feel well, fifty men dies here every day.

It took Dennison seven days to arrive at Andersonville, it probably took Thomas ten days, which would put him there around April 21st.

REPORTS FROM GEN. NATHAN B. FORREST, GEN. S.D. LEE, AND GEN. JAMES R. CHALMERS ON THE FORT PILLOW BATTLE.

FORREST'S letter to Lieutenant-General POLK, Demoplois, Alabama.
JACKSON, TENN.,
April 15, 1864.

GENERAL: I attacked Fort Pillow on the mourning of the 12th instant with a part of Bell's and McCulloch's brigades, numbering 1,500, under Brig. Gen. James R. Chalmers. After a short fight drove the enemy, 700 strong, into the fort under cover of their gunboats. Demanded a surrender, which was declined by Maj. L.F. Booth, commanding U.S. Forces. I stormed the fort, and after a contest of thirty minutes captured the entire garrison, killing 500 and taking 200 horses and a large amount of quartermaster's stores. The officers in the fort were killed, including Major Booth. I sustained a loss of 20 killed and 60 wounded. Among the wounded is the gallant Lieut. Col. Wiley M. Reed while leading the fifth Mississippi. Over 100 citizens who had fled to the fort to escape conscription ran into the river and were drowned. The Confederate flag now floats over the fort.

N.B.Forrest,
Major-General

FORREST'S letter to Lieut. Col. THOMAS M. JACK, Assistant Adjutant-General.
HEADQUARTERS FORREST'S CAVALRY,
Jackson, Tenn., April 15, 1864.

COLONEL: A dispatch of the 9th instant from lieutenant-general commanding reached me on the morning of the 13th at Fort Pillow. Orders were issued at once to have the same complied with. Brigadier-General Chalmers, commanding McColloch's and Bell's brigades, was ordered to make necessary preparations for moving to Okolona by way of Abbeville, that being the only route upon which forage could be obtained with facility. Col. J.J. Neely, commanding Richardson's brigade, was ordered to put himself in readiness to report to and follow General Chalmers as early as possible. Brigadier-General Buford, commanding one brigade in Kentucky, is ordered to this point, and will be here by Tuesday next (the 19th), when he will follow on also. They will proceed to Okolona and there report to you. I am in hopes to be able to come on at the same time, but am now suffering exhaustion, caused by hard riding and bruises received in the late enagagement (Fort Pillow). I will leave Colonel Duckworth's regiment and Lieutenant-Colonel Crew's battalion for the purpose of conscripting the State and holding guerrillas in check. You will please give such instructions as you may desire to my quartermaster and commisary, whom I ordered to remain at Aberdeen, that being a central point.

Please comminicate your instructions to me or Brigadier-General Chalmers at Okolona. Have dispatched by telegraph of the capture of Fort Pillow.

Arrived there on the morning of the 12th and attacked the place with a portion of McCulloch's and Bell's brigades numbering about 1,500 men, and after a sharp contest captured the garrison and allof its stores. A demand was made for the surrender, which was refused. The victory was complete, and the loss of the enemy will never be known from the fact that large numbers ran into the river and were shot and drowned. The force was composed of about 500 negroes and 200 white soldiers (Tennessee Tories). The river was dyed with the blood of the slaughtered for 200 yards. There was in the fort a large number of citizens who had fled there to escape the conscript law. Most of these ran into the river and were drowned. The approximate loss was upward of 500 killed, but few of the officers escaping.

It is hoped that these facts will demonstrate to the Northern people that negro soldiers cannot cope with Southerners. We still hold the fort.

My loss was about 20 killed and about 60 wounded. Among the latter I regret to state Lieut. Col. W.M. Reed, commanding George's regiment. He was shot in three places, and it is feared that his wounds may prove mortal. The country can ill afford to lose the services of so good and brave and officer at this time.— {he goes on to discuss other subjects}.

N.B. FORREST,
Major-General, Commanding.

Letter of congratulations from Brigadier-General, James R. Chalmers, to the soldiers who fought with him at Fort Pillow.
HDQRS. FIRST DIV., FORREST'S CAV. DEPT.,
Oxford, Miss., April 20, 1864.
SOLDIERS: I congratulate you upon your success in the brilliant campaign recently conducted in West Tennessee under the guidance of Major-General Forrest, whose star never shone brighter, and whose restless activity, untiring energy, and courage baffled the calculations and paralyzed the arms of our enemies.

In a brief space of time we have killed 4,000 of the enemy, captured over 1,200 prisoners, 800 horses, 5 pieces of artillary, thousands of small arms, and many stand of colors, destroyed millions of dollars worth of property, and relived the patriots of West Tennessee from the hourly dread in which they have been accustomed to live. West Tennessee is redeemed, and our friends who have heretofore been compelled to speak with bated breath now boldly proclaim their sentiments.

It is with pride and pleasure that I review the part taken by the soldiers of this division in this decisive campaign.

Colonel Duckworth, of the Seventh Tennessee, by a successful ruse at Union City made the enemy belive that Major-General Forrest was present, and compelled the surrender of the place by Hawkins and his regiment of renegade Tennesseeans, with all their arms, horses and equipments.

Colonel Neely, of the Thirteenth Tennessee, met the traitor Hurst at Bolivar, and after a short conflict, in which we killed and captured 75 prisoners of the enemy, drove Hurst hatless into Memphis, leaving in our hands all his wagons, ambulances, papers, and his mistresses, both black and white.

The once arrogant Grierson, who has never recovered his equanimity since his flight from Okolona, ventured out with two brigades to look after us, when Lieutenant-Colonel Crews, with his dashing battalion, defeated his advance gaurd, and sent him hurriedly back to Mamphis, where he remained trembling behind his fortifications and frightnened at every mention of the name Forrest.

Colonel Neely on the north and Colonel McGuirk on the south, by well-executed demonstrations, alarmed the enemy for the safety of Memphis, while lion-hearted McCulloch, with his "fighting brigade" of Missourians, Texans, and Mississippians, nobly assisted by Colonel Bell, with his gallant brigade of Tennesseeans, from Buford's division, temporarily attached to my command, stormed the works at Fort Pillow, in the face of the incessant fire from two gun-boats and five pieces of artillary from the fort, and taught the mongrel garrison of blacks and renegades a lesson long to be remembered.

While we rejoice over our victories, let us not forget the few gallant spirits who yielded up their lives to their country, and fell as brave men love to fall, "with their backs to the field and their feet to the foe,"

JAMES R. CHALMERS,
Brigadier-General, Commanding.

Report of Capt. John Goodwin, Provost-Marshal-General.
OKOLONA, MISS.,
April 21, 1864.

I accompany herewith list of prisoners captured by Major-General Forrest at Fort Pillow, as also one containing the names and owners and residences of the negroes captured at same place. Also is embraced a list of prisoners brought down from Jackson, Tenn., and no specific charges accompanying them; they will doubtless be sent in due time. F.P. Thomas is mentioned as a very bad man, he being among the number.

Also four stand of colors captured at Fort Pillow and one at another point. General Forrest wishes particular mention made of the large flag captured by Colonel Bell's brigade at Fort Pillow.

Yours, very resepctfully,
JNO. GOODWIN,
Provost-Marshal-General, General Forrest's Cav. Dept.

Letter from Lieutenant-General LEONIDAS POLK, to FORREST.
DEMOPOLIS, ALABAMA
April 24, 1864.
MAJOR-GENERAL FORREST,
Via Tupelo:
Your brilliant campaign in West Tennessee has given me great satisfaction, and entitles you to the thanks of your countrymen. Appropriate orders in writing will be transmitted you immediately. A movement of the enemy up the Yazoo has made it necessary that a division of your troops should move to meet it. I have ordered the brigade with General Chalmers and another from Okolona to move promptly so as to unite and give to General Adams the support he needs. I have also ordered Morton's battery to join them.

L. POLK
Lieutenant-General.

Letter from Gen. FORREST to Lieut. Col. THOMAS M. JACK, Assistant Adjutant-General.
HEADQUARTERS FORREST'S CAVALRY DEPARTMENT,
Jackson, Tenn., April 26, 1864.
COLONEL: I have the honor respectfully to forward you the following report of my engagem,ent with the enemy on the 12th instant at Fort Pillow:
My command consisted of McCulloch's brigade, of Chalmers' division, and Bell's brigade, of Buford's division, both placed for the expedition under command of Brig.

Gen. James R. Chalmers, who, by a forced march, drove the enemy's pickets, gained possession of the outer works, and by the time I reached the field, at 10 a.m., had forced the enemy tot heir main fortifications, situated on the bluff or bank of the Mississippi River at the mouth of Coal Creek. The fort is an earth-work, cresent shaped, is 8 feet in height and 4 feet across the top, surrounded by a ditch 6 feet deep and 12 feet in width, walls sloping tot he ditch but perpindicular inside. It was garrisoned by 700 troops with six pieces of artillary. A deep ravine surrounds the fort, and from the fort to the ravine the ground descends rapidly. Assuming command, I ordered General Chalmers to advance his lines and gain position on the slope, where our men would be perfectly protected from the heavy fire of artillary and musketry, as the enemy could not depress their pices so as to rake the slopes, nor could they fire on them with small-arms except by mounting the breast-works and exposing themselves to the fire of our sharpshooters, who, under cover of stumps and logs, forced them to keep down inside the works.

After several hours hard fighting the desired position was gained, not however, without considerable loss. Our main line was now within an average distance of 100 yards from the fort, and extended from Coal Creek, on the right, to the bluff, or bank, of the Mississippi River on the left.

During the entire morning the gun-boat kept up a continued fire in all directions, but without effect, and being confident of my ability to take the fort by assault, and desiring to prevent further loss of life, I sent, under flag of truce, a demand for uncoditional surrender of the garrison, a copy of which demand is hereto appended, marked No. 1, to which I received a reply, marked No. 2. The gun-boat had ceased firing, but the smoke of three other boats ascending the river was in view, the foremost boat apparently crowded with troops, and believing the request for an hour was to gain time for re-enforcements to arrive, and that the desire improperly to communicate with her, I at once sent this reply, copy of which is numbered 3, directing Captain Goodman, assistant adjutant-general of Brigadier-General Chalmers, who bore the flag, to remain until he received a reply or until the expiration of the time proposed.

My dispositions had all been made, and my forces were in position that would enable me to take the fort with less loss than to have to withdrawn under fire, and it seemed to me so perfectly apparent to the garrison that such was the case, that I deemed their capture without further bloodshed a certanty. After some little delay, seeing a message delivered to Captain Goodman, I rode up myself to where the notes were received and delivered. The answer handed me, written in pencil on a slip of paper, without envelope, and was, as well as I remember, in these words: "Negotiations will not attain the desired object." As the officers who were in charge of the Federal flag of truce had expressed a doubt as to my presence, and had pronaounced the demand a trick, I handed them back the note saying: "I am General Forrest; go back and say to Major Booth that I demand an answer in plain, unmistakable English. Will he fight or surrender?" Returning to my original position, before the expiration of twenty minutes I received a reply, copy of which is marked No. 4.

While these negotiations were pending the steamers from below were rapidly approaching the fort. The foremost was the Olive Branch, whose position and movements indicated her intention to land. A few shots fired into her caused her to leave the shore and make for the opposite. One other boat passed up on the far side of the river, the third one turned back.

The time having expired, I directed Brigadier-General Chalmers to prepare for the assault. Bell's brigade occupied the right, with his extreme right resting on Coal Creek.

McCulloch's brigade occupied the left, extending from the center of the river.

Three companies of his left regiment were placed in an old rifle-pit on the left and almost in the rear of the fort, which had evidently been thrown up for protection of sharpshooters or riflemen in supporting the water batteries below. On the right a portion of Barteau's regiment, of Bell's brigade, was also under the bluff and in rear of the fort. I dispatched staff officers to Colonel Bell and McCulloch, commanding brigades, to say to them that I should watch with interest the conduct of the troops; that Missourians, Mississippians, and Tennesseeans surrounded the works, and I desired to see who would first scale the fort. Fearing the gun-boats and transports might attempt a landing, I directed mu aide-de-camp, Capt. Charles W. Anderson, to assume command of the three companies on the left and rear of the fort and hold the position against anything that might come by land or water, but to take no part in the assault on the fort. Everything being ready, the bugle sounded the charge, which was made with a yell, and the works carried without a perceptible halt in any part of the line. As our troops mounted and poured into the fortification the enemy retreated toward the river, arms in hand and firing back, and their colors flying, no doubt expecting the gun-boat to shell us away from the bluff and protect them until they could be taken off or re-enforced. As they descended the bank an enfilading and deadly fire was pouired into them by the troops under Captain Anderson, on the left, and Barteu's detachment on the right. Until this fire was opened upon them, at a distance varying from 30 to 100 yrads, they were evidnelty ignorant of any force having gained their rear. The regiment who had stormed and carried the fort also poured a destuctive fire into the rear of the retreating and now panic-striken and almost decimated garrison. Fortunately for those of the enemy who survived this short but desperate struggle, some of our men cut the halyards, and the United States flag, floating from a tall mast in the center of the fort, came down. The forces stationed in the rear of the fort could see the flag, but were to far under the bluff to se the fort, and when the flag descended they ceased firing. But for this, so near were they to the enemy that few, if any, would have survived unhurt another volley. As it was, many rushed into the river and were drowned, and the actual loss of life will perhaps never be known, as there were a quite a number of refugee citizens in the fort, many of whom were drowned and several killed in the retreat from the fort. In less than twenty minutes from the time the bugles sounded the charge firing had ceased and the work done. One of the Parrott guns was turned on the gun-boat. She steamed off without replying. She had, as I afterward understood, expended all her ammunition, and was therefore powerless in affording the Federal garrison the aid and protection they doubtless expected of her when they retreated toward the river. Details were made, consisting of captured Federals and negroes, in charge of their own officers, to collect together and bury the dead, which work continued until dark.

I also direct Captain Anderson to procure a skiff and take with him Captain Young, a captured Federal officer, and deliver to Captain Marshall, of the gun-boat, the message, copy of which is appended and numbered 5. All boats and skiffs having been taken off by citizens escaping from the fort during the engagement, the message could not be delivered, although every effort was made to induce Captain Marshall to send his boat ashore by raising a white flag, with which Captain Young walked up and down the river in vain signaling her to come in or send out a boat. She finally moved off and disappeared around the bend above the fort. General Chalmers withdrew his forces from the fort before dark and encamped a few miles east of it.

On the morning of the 13th, I again dispatched Captain Anderson to Fort Pillow for the purpose of placing, if possible, the Federal wounded on board their transports, a report to me on his return the condition of affairs at the river. I respectfully refer you his report, numbered 6.

My loss in the engagement was 20 killed and 60 wounded. That of the enemy unknown. Two hundred and twenty eight were buried on the evening of the battle, and quite a number were buried the next day by details from the gun-boat fleet.

We captured 6 pieces of artillary, viz., two 10-pounder Parrott guns, two 12-pounder howitzers, and two brass 6-pounder guns, and about 350 stand of small-arms. The balance of the small-arms had been thrown in the river. All the small-arms were picked up where the enemy fell or threw them down. A few were in the fort, the balance scattered from the top of the hill to the water's edge.

We captured 164 Federals, 75 negro troops, and about 40 negro women and children, and after removing everything of value as far as able to do so, the warehouses, tents, &c., were destroyed by fire.

Among our severly wounded id Lieut. Col. Wiley M. Reed, assigned temporarily to the command of the Fifth Mississippi Regiment, who fell severly wounded while leading his regiment. When carried from the field he was supposed to be mortally wounded, but hopes are entertained of his ulimate recovery. He is a brave and gallant officer, a courteous gentelman, and a consistant Christian minister.

I cannot compliment too highly the conduct of Colonels Bell and McCulloch and the officers and men of their brigades, which composed the forces of Brigadier-General Chalmers. They fought with courage and interpidity, and without bayonets assaulted and carried one of the strongest fortifications in the country.

On the 15th, at Brownsville, I received orders which rendered it necessary to send General Chalmers, in command of his own division and Ball's brigade, southward; hence I have no offical report from him, but will, as soon as it can be obtained, forward a complete list of our killed and wounded, which has been ordered made out and forwarded at the earliest possible moment.

In closing my report I desire to ackowledge the prompt and energetic action of Brigadier-General Chalmers, commanding the forces around Fort Pillow. His faithful execution of all movements necessary to the successful accomplishment of the object of the expedition entitles him to special mention. He has reason to be proud of the conduct of the officers and men of his command for their gallantry and courage in assualting and carrying the enemy's work without the assistance of artillary or bayonets.

To my staff, as heretofor, my acknowledgements are due for their prompt and faithful delivery of all orders.

I am, colonel, very respectfully, your obedient servant,

N.B. FORREST,

Major-General, Commanding.

Report of Brig. Gen. James R. Chalmers, C.S. Army, commanding First Division Cavalry, of the capture of Fort Pillow.

HDQRS. FIRST DIVISION, FORREST'S CAV. DEPARTMENT,

Verona, May 7, 1864.

MAJOR: I have the honor to submit the following report of the actions of the troops under my command in the recent capture of Fort Pillow, Tenn.:

in obedience to orders from Major-General Forrest, I directed Col. J.J. Neely, commanding First Brigade of this division, to move his command, on the morning of the 10th April, from whiteville southward in the direction of Memphis, instructing him to produce the impression thet he was the advance of General Forrest's command, and that our whole force was in his rear, and to make preparations for constructing pontoon bridges across Wolf River at Raleigh and one or two other points, and to make such demonstrations as would induce the enemy to believe that our whole force was about to attack Memphis. At the same time I ordered Col. John McGuirk, Third Regiment Mississippi State Cavalry, to move with his own regiment and the First Mississippi Partisans, under Major Park, northward from the Tallahatchie River toward Memphis, and to report that Major-General Lee was advancing from the north of that place. It gives me pleasure to report that both of these officers executed these orders with promptness and success.

I then assumed command of a division composed of McCulloch's brigade of my division and Col. T.H. Bell's brigade of Buford's division.

On the morning of the 11th instant, I moved this division from Sharon's Ferry, on Forked Deer, in the direction of Brownsville, and on the same morning moved Lieutenant-Colonel Chalmers' battalion through Brownsville on the Memphis road, and thence by a circuitous route back again to the Fort Pillow road. I moved from Brownsville in person, at 3:30 p.m., on the 11th and reached Fort Pillow, a distance of 40 miles, at daylight next morning.

Colonel McCulloch, commanding advance, surprised the enemy's pickets and captured 4 of them. My orders from General Forrest were to invest the place, and I proceeded to do so as follows: McCulloch's brigade moved down the Fulton road to Gaine's farm; thence north to the fort on a road running parallel with the Mississippi River; Wilson's regiment, of Bell's brigade, moved on the direct road from Brownsville to Fort Pillow, and Colonel Bell with Barteau's and Russell's regiments moved down Coal Creek to attack the fort in the rear.

The works at Fort Pillow consisted of a strong line of fortifications, originally constructed by Brigadier-General Pillow, of the C.S. Army, stretching from Coal Creek bottom, on the left, to the Mississippi River on the right, in length about 2 miles and at an average distance of about 600 yards from the river. Inside of this outer line and about 600 yards from it stood and interior work on the crest of a commanding hill, originally commenced by Brigadier-General Villepigue, C.S. Army, which covered about 2 acres of ground. About 300 yards in rear of this, above the junction of Coal Creek and the Mississippi River, stood the last fortification, which was a strong dirt fort in semicircular form. with a ditch in front of it 12 feet wide and 8 feet deep.

The enemy did not attempt to hold the outer line, but trained their artillary so as to play upon the only roads leading through it. The fight was opened at daylight by McCulloch. He moved cautiously through the ravines and short hills which incompassed the place, protecting the men as much as possibe from the enemy's artillary, five pieces of which the fort, aided by two gun-boats on the river, played furiously upon him. Moving in this manner he succeeded about 11 o'clock in taking the work, which I have spoken of as been commenced by General Villepigue, and the flag of the eighteenth Mississippi Battalion, Lieutenant-Colonel Chalmers commanding, which had been the first regiment to enter the fort, was quickly flying above it.

While Colonel McCulloch had been moving up on the left, Colonel Bell moved up on the right and rear, and Colonel Wilson moved up on the center, taking advantage of the ground as much as possible to shelter their men. Affairs were in this condition, with the main fort completely invested, when Major-General Forrest arrived with Colonel Wisdom's regiment of Buford's division. after carefully examining the position he ordered a general charge to be made. The troops responded with alacrity and enthusiasm, and in a short itme took possesion of all the rifle-pits around the fort, and closed up on all sides within 25 or 30 yards of the outer ditch. Here a considerable delay occured from the ammunition being exhausted. A supply, however, was obtained as quickly as possible from the ordinance train and everything was made ready for another advance.

To prevent the unnecessary effusion of blood Major-General Forrest now demanded, under flag of truce, the surrender of the place, which after a parley of about thirty minutes was refused. The bugle then sounded the charge, a general rush was made along the whole line, and in five minutes the ditch was crossed, the parapet scaled, and our troops were in possession of the fort.

The enemy made no attempt to surrender, no white flag was elevated, nor was the U.S. flag lowered until pulled down by our men. Many of them were killed while fighting, and many more in the attempt to escape. The strength of the enemy's force cannot be correctly ascertained, though it was probably about 650 or 700. Of these 69 wounded were delivered to the enemy's gun-boats next day, after having been paroled. One hundred and sixty-four white men and 40 negroes were taken prisoners, making an aggregate of 273 prisoners. It is probable as many as half a dozen may have escaped. The remainder of the garrison killed.

I cannot speak too highly of the conduct of the troops under my command. Colonels McCulloch and Bell deserve especial mention for the gallantry with which they led there respective brigades, and the troops emulated the conduct of their leaders. Lieutenant-Colonel Reed, temporarily commanding the Fifth Mississippi Cavalry, was preeminently daring, and fell mortally wounded while standing on the rifle-pits and encouraging his men to the charge, and Lieutenant Burton was killed at his side. Lieutenant Ryan, of Willis's Texas Battalion, who had won fro himself the character of being the best soldier in his regiment, was killed by a shell, and Captain Sullivan, commanding the same battalion, was mortally wounded while most gallantly leading his command. Lieutenant Hubbard, of the Eighteenth Mississippi Battalion, a young but promising officer, was mortally wounded and has since died.

I cannot conclude this report without montioning in an especial manner the gallant conduct of Capt. C.T. Smith, commanding my escort, who was killed in the charge.

I have already furnished a detailed report of the killed and wounded of my command, amounting to 14 killed and 86 wounded. A report of captured property had been called for from the two brigades, and will be forwarded as soon as received.

I herewith submit reports of subordinate commanders.

I have the honor to be, major, very respectfully, your obedient servant,

JAMES R. CHALMER,

Brigadier-General, Commanding.

JOINT RESOLUTION Of thanks to Maj. Gen. N.B. Forrest and the officers and men of his command, for their campaign in Mississippi, West Tennessee, and Kentucky.

Resolved by the Congress of the Confederate States of America,

That the thanks of Congress are eminently due, and are hereby cordially tendered, to Maj. Gen. N.B. Forrest, and the officers and men of his command, for their late brilliant and successful campaign in Mississippi, West Tennessee, and Kentucky-a campaign has conferred upon its authors fame as enduring as the records of the struggle which they have so brilliantly illustrated.

Approved, May 23, 1864.

Page

Reports of Lieut. Gen. Stephen D. Lee, C.S. Army, Conmmanding Department of Alabama. Mississippi, and East Louisiana, of the capture of Fort Pillow, etc., to Genral S. Cooper, Adjutant and Inspector General, C.S. Army, Richmond, Va.

HDQRS. DEPARTMENT ALA., MISS., AND EAST LA.,

Meridian, Miss., May 27, 1864.

GENERAL: I have the honor to forward herewith, by Col. T.W. White, Ninth Mississippi Regiment, 1 flag captured from the enemy at Union city, Tenn., and 4 garrison flags and 8 guidons captured at Fort Pillow, Tenn., all by Maj. Gen N.B. Forrest's cavalry command in April last.

It would be superfluous fro me here to advert to the skill and gallantry displayed by Maj. Gen. N.B. Forrest and the officers and men under his command in the engagements above referred to, in which such a handsome addition has been made to the trophies we have wrested from the enemy. Few cavalry raids have been productive of such brilliant results to our arms or of such disastrous discomfiture to the enemy as that which was rendered famous the expedition whence General Forrest's command has just returned. I will direct that Union city and Fort Pillow be inscribed on the colors of those orginizations which distinguished themselves in these engagements.

I am, general, yours, respectfully,

S.D. LEE,

Major-General, Commanding Department.

GENERAL CORRESPONDENCE AND UNION TESTIMONY TO THE FORT PILLOW BATTLE

The following is the majority of Union correspondence and testimonies collected in the Official Records Of The Civil War concerning the battle at Fort Pillow.

HDQRS. U.S. COLORED TROOPS IN TENNESSEE,
Memphis, Tenn., April 14, 1864.
 Hon. E.B. WASHBURNE,
 Washington, D.C.:
 MY DEAR SIR: Before this letter reaches you, you will have learned of the capture of Fort Pillow and the slaughter of our troops after the place was captured. This is the most infernal outrage that has been committed since the war began. Three weeks ago I sent up four companies of colored troops to that place under Major Booth, a most brave and efficient [officer], who took command of the post. Forrest and Chalmers, with about 3,000 devils, attacked the place on the 12th at 9 a.m. and succeeded after three assaults, and when both Major Booth and Major Bradford, of the Thirteenth Tennessee Cavalry, had been killed, in capturing the place at 4 p.m. We had, in all, less than 500 effective men, and one-third of whom were colored.
 The colored troops fought with desperation throughout. After the capture our colored men were literally butchered. Chalmers was present and saw it all. Out of 300 colored men, not 25 were taken prisoners, and they may have been killed long before this.
 There is a great deal of excitement in town in consequence of this affair, especially among our colored troops. If this is to be the game of the enemy they will soon learn that it is one at which two can play.
 The Government will no doubt take cognizance of this matter immediately and take such measures as will prevent a recurrence.
 It is reported that Forrest will move on this place in a few days. I do not believe it. I am hurried and can write no more to-day. I am feeling dreadfully over the fate of my brave officers and men. Like all others, I feel that the blood of these heroes must be avenged.
 Forrest will probably try to get out of West Tennessee as soon as he can. We have reinforcements coming in, and we shall soon be on his track.
 In haste, sincerely, your friend,
 CHETLAIN,
 Brigadier-General.

HDQRS. MILITARY DIVISION OF THE MISSISSIPPI
Nashville, Tenn., April 15, 1864. (Received 2.30 p.m.)
 Lieutenant-General GRANT,
 Culpepper, Va.:
 General Braymen reports from Cairo the arrival of 50 wounded white soldiers from Fort Pillow, and that the place was attacked on the 12th, 50 white soldiers killed and 100 taken prisoners, and 300 blacks murdered after surrender. I dont know what these men were doing at Fort Pillow. I ordered it to be abandoned before I went to Meridian, and it was so abandoned. General Hurlbut must have sent this garrison up recently

from Memphis. So many men are on furlough that Grierson and Hurlbut seem to fear going out of Memphis to attack Forrest. I have no apprehension for the safety of Paducah, Columbus, or Memphis, but without drawing from Dodge, I have no force to send over there, and dont want to interrupt my plans of preparation for the great object of the spring campaign. I expect McPherson's two divisions from Vicksburg to rendezvous at Cairo from furlough about the 20th, and I look for A.J. Smith up daily from Red River. Whenever either of these commands arrive I can pen Forrest up, but it will take some time to run him down. Do you want me to delay for such a purpose, but shall I go on to concentrate on Chattanooga?

I dont know what to do with Hurlbut. I know that Forrest could pen him up in Memphis with 2,500 men, although Hurlbut has all of Grierson's Cavalry and 2,500 white infantry, 4,000 blacks, and the citizen militia, 3,000. If you think I have time I will send a division from Dodge to Purdy, and order A.J. Smith as he comes up to strike inland to Boliver, Jackson, &c., and come across by land to Tennessee. This may consume and extra two weeks.

Corse was at Vicksburg ready to start up the Red River the 8th.

W.T. SHERMAN,
Major-General.

CULLPEPPER VA.,
April 15, 1864 - 8 p.m.

Major-General Sherman:

Forrest must be driven out, but with a proper commander in West Tennessee, there is force enough now. Your preparations for the coming campaign must go on, but if it is necessary to detach a portion of the troops intended for it, detach them and make your campaign with that much fewer men.

Relieve Maj. Gen. Hurlbut. I can send General Washburn, a sober and energetic officer, to take his place. I can also send you General L.C. Hunt to command District of Columbus. Shall I send Washburn? Does General Hurlbut think if he moves a part of his force after the only enemy within 200 miles of him that the post will run off with the balance of his force?

If our men have been murdered after capture, retaliation must be resorted to promptly.

U.S. Grant,
Lieutenant-General.

HDQRS. MILITARY DIVISION OF THE MISSISSIPPI,
Nashville, Tenn., April 23, 1864.

Hon. E.M. STANTON,
Secretary of War, Washington:

Sir: Pursuant to your orders two officers are now engaged in taking affidavits and collecting testimony as to the Fort Pillow affair. They are ordered to send you direct, a copy of their report and one to me.

I know well the animus of the Southern soldiery, and truth is they cannot be restrained. The effect will be of course to make the Negroes desperate, and when in turn they commit horrid acts of retaliation we will be relieved of responsibility. Thus far Negroes have been comparatively well behaved, and have not committed the horrid excesses and barbarities which the Southern papers much dreaded.

I send you herewith my latest newspapers from Atlanta, of the 18th and 19th instant.

W.T. Sherman   *Lieutenant General U.S. Grant*

In them you will find articles of interest and their own accounts of the Fort Pillow affair.

The enemy will contend that a place taken by assault is not entitled to quarter, but this rule would have justified us in an indiscriminate slaughter at Arkansas Post, Fort De Russy, and other places taken by assault. I doubt the wisdom of any fixed rule by our Government, but let soldiers affected make their own rules as we progress. We will use their own logic against them, as we have from the beginning of the war.

The Southern army, which is the Southern people, cares no more for our clamor than the idle wind, but they will heed the slaughter that will follow as the natural consequence of their own inhuman acts.

I am, &c.,

W.T. SHERMAN,

Major-General, Commanding.

HEADQUARTERS DISTRICT OF CAIRO,

Cairo, Ill., April 28, 1864.

Hon. E.M. STANTON,

Secretary of War, Washington:

Sir: Having been so instructed by Major-General Sherman, commanding the Military Division of the Mississippi, I have the honor to transmit such testimony as I have been able to procure relative to the late tragedy at Fort Pillow.

In some cases the reports of commissioned officers have been received without oath, but nearly all the statements are sworn to in the usual manner.

Many persons who could have testified fully are not now accessible, having separated.

Recognizing the exigency of the case, I prefer to transmit such as could be obtained in the shortest time;. With your approbation "I will add such as an be hereafter procured.

You will, however, find sufficient in these papers to enforce absolute conviction upon all minds that violations of the laws and usage's of civilized war, and those obligations of common humanity which even barbarous and heathen tribes in some sort observe, have been perpetrated.

Men and women who passed through the excitements of the battle, as well as the horrors of an indiscriminate massacre, which raged not only when the blood was hot and the judgment clouded by conflict, but which reached into the quiet of the following day, most of them mutilated, hacked, and torn, and some while dying, have patiently, calmly, and even with forgiving sprit, told their pitiful story. The solemnities of an oath under such circumstances would seem to be scarcely required.

It may be added that these murders came not of sudden heat, consequent upon battle and perpetrated by soldiers whom their officers could not control. The purpose to do this very thing was avowed beforehand by rebel officers in command. At Paducah threats of indiscriminate murder were made; at Columbus the slaughter of all colored soldiers was threatened. These threats were made in official papers signed by the generals in command, and which are in our possession. Verbal threats of the same character will in due time be proven. By the casualty of war the fate intended for Paducah and Columbus fell only upon Fort Pillow.

A full and formal report of military operations within this district since I had the honor to be assigned to its command will be forwarded at the [end] of this month, to which reference is made for closer details.

Very respectfully, your obedient servant,

M. BRAYMAN,

Brigadier-General, Commanding.

Testimony of Ransom Anderson (colored), private in Company B, Sixth U.S. Heavy Artillery:

I do hereby certify that I am a member of Company B, Sixth U.S. Heavy Artillery, and that I was in the battle of Fort Pillow on the 12th day of April, A.D. 1864, and that I was severely wounded during the progress of the engagement. When the surrender occurred I was taken prisoner. I also certify that while a prisoner and wounded I was further wounded by being cut in the head and hands by one Lieutenant Williams, C.S. Army. I also certify that I saw John Pritchard, of Company B, Sixth U.S. Heavy Artillery, shot while a prisoner and while lying by my side upon the ground.

I also certify that I saw Coolie Pride, of the same regiment and the same company, stabbed by a rebel solider with a bayonet and the bayonet broken off in his body, after the said Coolie Pride had been taken prisoner by the Confederates. On the mourning of the 13th day of April, A.D. 1864, after he had been taken prisoner, I saw Daniel Lester shot dead by a rebel solider.

Mound City, April 23, 1864

RANSOM (his x mark) ANDERSON.

Witness:

JOHN H. BAKER,

Captain Company B, Sixth U.S. Heavy Artillery.

Sworn and subscribed to before me this 23d day of April, 1864, at Mound City, Ill.

WM. STANLEY,

Lieutenant and Provost-Marshal.

CAIRO, ILL.,

April 23, 1864.

Elois Bevel, being duly sworn, deposes and says:

I am a citizen of Osceola, Ark. I was driven from my home by guerrillas. I arrived at Fort Pillow, Tenn., on the night of the 11th of April, 1864. I was at Fort Pillow during the engagement between the rebel forces under Forrest and Chalmers and the United States garrison at the place on the 12th instant, 1864. About sun-up the alarm of rebels being in the fort was received at Major Booth's headquarters. I took a position where I could see all further saith: I saw the contraband camps in flames at different points; could see the skirmishers of the rebels.

Signals were given by Captain Bradford to Captain Marshall, of the Navy, commanding gun-boat no. 7, to shell them from post No. 1, which was in sight of the fort, which was done by Captain Marshall. About one hour after sunrise brisk skirmishing began. The bullets from rebel infantry caused me to move from where I was and take position behind a large stump near the fort where I could better see the rebels who swarmed the bluff. The rebels were so near the gun-boat that the crew under Captain Marshall had to close their ports and use their small-arms. At 1 p.m. the firing on both sides ceased; a flag of truce was sent from the rebel lines to demand an unconditional surrender. While the flag of truce was approaching the fort I saw a battery of artillery moved to a better position by the rebels, and saw their sharpshooters approaching the fort from another quarter. At 2 o'clock the fight began again; about fifteen or twenty minutes after, I saw a charge made by about 2,000 on the breast-works, and near it on the bluff.

Sharp fighting took place inside the fort of about five minutes duration. I saw their bayonets and swords. I saw the Union soldiers, black and white slaughtered while asking for quarter; heard their screams for quarter, to which the rebels paid no attention. About 100 left the fort and ran down the bank of the bluff to the river, pursued by the rebels, who surrounded them. In about twenty minutes every one of them, as far as I could see, was shot down by rebels without mercy. I left at this time, getting on the gun-boat. On Thursday, the 14th of April, I met Captain Farris, of Forrest's command, about 6 miles from Fort Pillow, at Plum Point; his soldiers said they were hunting for Negroes. I asked him if they took any prisoners at Fort Pillow. He said they took some of the Thirteenth Tennessee, who surrendered, but no others.

ELOIS BEVEL.

Signed and sworn to before me this 23d day of April, A.D. 1864,

at Cairo, Ill.

C.B. SMITH,

Lieutenant and Acting Assistant Adjutant-General.

James R. Bingham, a resident of Fredonia, Chautauqua County,

N.Y., deposes and says:

He was, and has been, a clerk in a store at Fort Pillow over a year previous to the 12th April instant. On learning early in the mourning of the 12th instant that the post was to be attacked by the Confederates he went immediately to the fort, and was engaged with a musket in defending the fort when General Chalmers was repulsed twice.

After this I was detailed to carry wounded down the hill, on which the fort was situated, to the river bank, where, beside a large log, I raised a red flag as a sign of a hospital—the flag was made from part of a red flannel shirt. The last attack was made by General Forrest in person, who headed the column. Forrest was wounded in three places, and his horse shot under him.

Major Booth, of the regular army, was in command. He was killed about 11 o'clock by a sharpshooter, when Major Bradford, of the Thirteenth Tennessee Regiment, took command. Major Bradford was taken prisoner and killed, near judge Green's, some 6 miles from the fort, while a prisoner.

When the Confederates rushed into the fort—having taken advantage of a flag of truce to get their men close to the fort in a ravine, and directly under the embank-ments—this force numbered some 1,500 with a large reserve in sight. As soon as the Confederates got into the fort the Federals threw down their arms in token of surrender, and many exclaimed, "We surrender." Immediately an indiscriminate massacre com-menced on both black and white soldiers. Up to the time of the surrender I dont think more than from 20 to 25 had been killed, and not more than 15 wounded.

I was taken prisoner and when marching with other prisoners, black and white, I saw the Confederates shoot and kill wound both black and white prisoners. Some Ne-groes were severely beaten, but still able to go along. We were taken a few miles into the country, when myself and a few others got relieved by general McCulloch, on the ground of being private citizens.

I saw General Forrest, and knew he was wounded, as before stated. There were from 25 to 30 black soldiers carried off as prisoners, and not over 30 to 35 whites; all the rest of that faithful and heroic garrison, some 500 or 600 number, were killed and wounded in action, or murdered or wounded after the surrender. I saw officers as well as privates kill and wound prisoners, and heard them say, while held prisoner with them in the country, that they intended taking the prisoners still farther into the country and making an example of them.

Captain Bradford, of the Thirteenth Tennessee, was engaged with a blue signal flag, in connection with gun-boat No. 7. Captain Bradford was ordered shot by General Forrest, who said, "shoot that man with the black flag." This was after the surrender. His body was literally shot to pieces. All, both black and white, fought manfully. I saw several Negroes wounded, with blood running from their bodies, still engaged loading and firing cannon and muskets cheerfully.

There was no giving way till 1,500 Confederates rushed inside the fort; most were killed outside the fort when prisoners. The fort was defended successfully for eight hours by from 500 to 600 men against 3,500 to 4,000 barbarians. I heard Confederate officers say it was the hardest contested engagement that Forrest had ever been en-gaged in. I heard officers say they would never recognize Negroes as prisoners of war, but would kill them whenever taken; even if they caught a Negro with blue clothes on (uniform) they would kill him. Officers of Negro troops were treated and murdered the same as the Negroes themselves. After lying in the woods two days and nights, I was picked up by gun-boat No. 7, some 5 or 6 miles below the fort. On my return to the fort I saw and recognized the remains of Lieutenant Ackerstrom. He had been nailed to a house, and supposed burned alive. There were the remains of 2 Negroes lying where the house burned. I was told they were nailed to the floor. I also found a Negro partially buried with his head out of the ground alive. I went for assistance and water for him.

When I returned he was so near dead that no assistance could save him. We sat by until he died.

I cannot recount but a small part of the barbarities I saw on that fatal day, when hundreds of loyal soldiers were murdered in cold blood.

JAS. R. BINGHAM.

Sworn before me at Cairo, Ill., this 18th day of April, 1864.

JNO. H. MUNROE,

Assistant Adjutant-General.

Testimony of Hardin Cason, Company A, Sixth U.S. Heavy Artillery:

I do hereby certify that I was in the engagement at Fort Pillow, Tenn., on the 12th day of April, A.D. 1864, and that I was wounded during the battle and then taken prisoner. I also certify that on the following morning (being morning of the 13th of April, A.D. 1864) I saw Corpl. Robert Winston murdered by a rebel solider, Corporal Winston having been previously wounded during the progress of the battle on the 12th. I also certify that I saw several other men shot who had been taken prisoners, their names not being known by me.

Mound City, April 23, 1864.

HARDIN (his x mark) CASON.

Witness:

John H. BAKER,

Capt. Co. B., Sixth U.S. Heavy Artillery (colored).

Sworn and subscribed to before me this 23d day of April, 1864,

at Mound City, Ill.

WM. STANLEY,

Lieutenant and Provost-Marshal, Mound City.

Testimony of Corpl. Eli Cothel, Company B, Sixth U.S. Heavy Artillery:

I do hereby certify that I was wounded during the engagement at Fort Pillow, Tenn., on the 12th day of April, A.D. 1864. I was shot through the arm while thus a prisoner to the rebel forces. I saw 17 men thus shot, not knowing their names, after being taken prisoners.

Mound City, Ill., April 23, 1864.

ELI (his x mark) COTHEL.

Witness:

JOHN H. BAKER,

Capt. Co. B, Sixth U.S. Heavy Artillery (colored).

Sworn and subscribed to before me this 23d day of April, 1864, at Mound City, Ill.

WM. STANLEY,

Lieutenant and Assistant Provost-Marshal.

Statement of Corpl. William A. Dickey, Company B, Thirteenth Tennessee Cavalry:

I do hereby certify that I was at Fort Pillow, Tenn., on the 12th day of April, A.D. 1864, when that place was attacked by the rebel General Forrest. I went into the fort at the commencement of the action. We kept up continual fire upon both sides until about 1 p.m., when a flag of truce was sent in by the rebels, and while it was being considered the firing was ordered to cease, I also certify that while this was going on I plainly saw the enemy consolidating their forces and gaining positions they had been endeavoring to gain without success. At the same time their men were plundering our deserted camp, and stealing goods from the quartermaster's depot, and from the stores of the merchants of the post. They also at the same time put their sharpshooters into our deserted barracks, whence they had fair view and were in fair range of our little garrison. The firing recommenced after the flag of truce had retired. About one hour thereafter the rebels stormed our works. They had no sooner obtained the top of our walls when the Negroes ran, and the whites, obtaining no quarter, ran after them. The rebels followed closely, shooting down all who came in the way, white and black. I also certify that I myself was shot by a rebel soldier after I had surrendered, and while I had my hands up begging for mercy. I also certify that I saw the rebels shoot down 10 men, white soldiers, within 10 paces of me while they had their hands up supplicating quarter. I also certify that I saw 12 Negro soldiers killed long after they had surrendered. I also certify that I saw rebels throw several Negroes into the river while they were begging for life.

One rebel came to me and took my percussion caps, saying he had been killing Negroes so fast that his own had been exhausted; he added that he was going to shoot some more. I also certify that I saw Negroes thrown into the river by rebels, and shot afterward, while struggling for life.

Mound City, April 23, A.D. 1864.

WM. A. (his x mark) DICKEY.

Witness:

WILLIAM CLEARY,

Second Lieut. Co. B, Thirteenth Tenn. Vol. Cavalry.

Sworn and subscribed to before me the 25th day of April, 1864, at Mound City, Ill.

WM. STANLEY,

Lieutenant and Assistant Provost-Marshal.

Testimony of Elias Falls, Company A, Sixth U.S. Heavy Artillery:

I do hereby certify that I was in the battle of Fort Pillow on the 12th day of April, A.D. 1864, and that I was taken prisoner. I was ordered with several others to march up the hill, and we were fired upon while thus marching. I was the second man shot while in the hands of the rebel officers, and obeying their commands while marching up the hill. Several others, to my certain knowledge, were shot by the rebels on this occasion.

Mound City, Ill., April 23, 1864.

ELIAS (his x mark) FALLS.

Witness:

JOHN H. BAKER,

Captain Co. B, Sixth U.S. Heavy Artillery (colored).

Sworn and subscribed to before me this 23d day of April, 1864, at Mound City, Ill.

WM. STANLEY,

Lieutenant and Assistant Provost-Marshal.

Statement of Jason Souden, Company B, Thirteenth Tennessee Cavalry:

I do hereby certify that I was at Fort Pillow, Tenn., on the 12th of the present month, when it was attacked by rebels under General N.B. Forrest. I was ordered into the fort at the commencement of the engagement. We kept up a continual fire on both sides until about 1 p.m., when a flag of truce was sent in and firing ceased. While the flag of truce was being considered, I saw the enemy plundering our evacuated quarters and moving their forces in bodies, getting them in position. We had been driving them all mourning. They were at the same time placing their sharpshooters in the buildings we had occupied as barracks. The object of the flag of truce not having been agreed to, the firing again commenced. About one hour afterward the enemy charged on our works in overwhelming numbers, and the Negro soldiers being panic-stricken dropped their arms and ran down the bluff. The whites also, when they found there was no quarter shown, also ran down the bluff. The rebels ran after us shooting all they came to, both black and white. I also certify that I myself was shot after I had surrendered, and while I had my hands up and was imploring them to show me mercy. They also shot Sergeant Gwaltney, of my company, while he was within 10 feet of me, after he had given up his revolver, and while he had his hands up crying out for mercy. They took his own re-volver and shot him through with its contents twice through the head, killing him in-stantly. I also certify that I saw the rebels shoot in all 6 men who had surrendered, and who had their hands up asking for quarter. I further certify that I saw the rebels come about on the ensuing morning, the 13th day of April, A.D. 1864, and dispatch several of the colored soldiers of the Sixth U.S. Heavy Artillery, who had survived their wounds received on the previous day.

Mound City, Ill., April 23, 1864.

JASON (his x mark) SOUDEN.

Witness:

WILLIAM CLEARY,

Second Lieut. Co. B, Thirteenth Tennessee Cavalry.

Sworn and subscribed to before me this 25th day of April, 1864, at Mound City, Ill.

WM. STANLEY,

Lieutenant and Assistant Provost-Marshal.

Statement of William J. Mays, Company B, Thirteenth Tennessee Cavalry:

MOUND CITY, April 18, 1864.

I was at Fort Pillow on the 12th of April, 1864, and engaged in the fight there. The pickets were driven in about 6 a.m., when skirmishers were thrown out to ascertain the position and number of the enemy. The contraband camp was then discovered to be on fire, and the firing of small-arms was heard in the same direction. The skirmishing lasted about one hour, when our skirmishers were gradually driven back toward the fort on the bluff. They then attacked the fort. Two assaults were made by them, and both repulsed. This was about 11 or 12 a.m., when a flag of truce was sent in demanding surrender. While the flag was being received and the firing suspended the enemy were moving their forces into position, and occupied one position which they had been fighting to obtain all day but had not been able to gain except under the protection of a flag of truce. It was from this position they made their heaviest assault, it being impossible to bring our artillery to bear upon them. Question. Do you think they could have taken the fort or that particular position had they not done so under cover of the flag of truce?

Answer. I do not; they had been kept from it for six hours.

Question. What further took place? Go on with your statement. In about five min-utes after the disappearance of the flag of truce a general assault was made upon our works from every direction. They were kept at bay for some time, when the Negroes gave way upon the left and ran down the bluff, leaving an opening through which the rebels entered and immediately commenced and indiscriminate slaughter of both white and black. We all threw down our arms and gave tokens of surrender, asking for quarter (I was wounded in the right shoulder and muscle of the back and knocked down before I threw down my gun). But no quarter was given. Voices were heard upon all sides, crying, "give them no quarter; kill them; kill them; it is General Forrest's orders.' I saw 4 white and at least 25 Negroes shot while begging for mercy, and I saw 1 Negro dragged from a hollow log within 10 feet of where I lay, and as 1 rebel held by the foot another shot him. These were all soldiers. There were also 2 Negro women and 3 little children standing within 25 steps from me, when a rebel stepped up to them and said, "Yes, God damn you, you thought you were free, did you?" and shot them all. They all fell but 1 child, when he knocked it in the head with the breech of his gun. They then disappeared in the direction of the landing, following up the fugitives, firing at them wherever seen. They came back in about three-quarters of an hour, shooting and robbing the dead of their money and clothes. I saw a man with a canteen upon him and a pistol in his hand. I ventured to ask him for a drink of water.

He turned around, saying, "Yes, God damn you, I will give you a drink of water," and shot at my head three different times, covering my face up with dust, and then turned from me—no doubt thinking he had killed me—remarking, "God damn you, its to late to pray now;" then went on with his pilfering. I lay there until dark, feigning death, when a rebel officer came along drawing his saber, and ordered me to get up, threatening to run his saber into me if I did not, saying I had to march 10 miles that night. I succeeded in getting up and got among a small squad he had already gathered up, but stole away from them during the night and got among the dead, feigning death for fear of being murdered.

The next morning the gun-boat came up and commenced shelling them out, when I crawled out from among the dead and with a piece of paper motioning to the boat; she came up, and I crawled on board.

WM. J. (his x mark) MAYS.

Sworn and subscribed to before me this 27th day of April, 1864.

WM. STANLEY,

Lieutenant and Assistant Provost-Marshal.

Testimony of Emanuel Nichols, Company B, Sixth U.S. Heavy Artillery:

I do hereby certify that I was in the battle fought at Fort Pillow, Tenn., on the 12th day of April, A.D. 1864, and that I was wounded during the engagement, I also certify that after being wounded I was taken prisoner, and on the following morning, 13th of April, A.D. 1864, I was shot by a rebel soldier and left for dead upon the battlefield.

Mound City, Ill., April 23, A.D. 1864.

EMANUEL (his x mark) NICHOLS.

Witness:

JOHN H. BAKER,

Captain Co. B, Sixth U.S. Heavy Artillery (colored).

Sworn and subscribed to before me this 23d day of April, 1864, at Mound City, Ill.

WM. STANLEY,

Lieutenant and Provost-Marshal, Mound City, Ill.

MOUND CITY, April 25, 1864.

Statement of Daniel H. Rankin, Company C, Thirteenth Tennessee Cavalry Volunteers:

I was in Fort Pillow on Tuesday, the 12th of April, 1864, and was engaged in the fight there on that day. They drove in our pickets about 6 a.m. They came in as skirmishers and sharpshooters. This kind of fighting lasted some two hours, when we were driven into the fort, the rebels taking possession of our rifle-pits. The firing from both sides continued up to about 12 o'clock, they endeavoring to gain position from which to storm our works, but were unable. They made two different assaults, but were repulsed each time. They then sent in a flag of truce demanding a surrender of the works, which demand was refused. while the flag was in waiting and the firing suspended the rebels were moving for position, and actually occupied the one which they had endeavored to occupy all forenoon, but in vain, and the one from which the heaviest assault was made upon us in overwhelming numbers. We held them at bay for some time, when two companies of Negro troops broke and ran down the bluff, which made an opening for the rebels to come in at, when they got possession of our works and indiscriminate slaughter commenced of both white and black. When I saw we were overpowered I threw down my gun and took off my cartridge-box and asked for quarter. I heard an officer of some description order his men to kill us and show no quarter. I was standing at this time just under the bluff, and the rebels upon top firing at us. I held up my hands and told them I had surrendered, but they still kept firing. I was hit seven times after I had thrown down my arms in token of surrender, though some of the wounds were light. I was then taken prisoner. I was taken some 2 miles from the fort with the other prisoners, I think some 100 whites and some 10 or 20 Negroes. The next morning after the fight myself and some 10 or 12 other wounded were paroled and started into the fort. I started in company with two rebel surgeons, the others having gone before. As we started we heard firing, when one of the surgeons remarked that is some of our boys shooting down those wounded. I don't know whether it was done or not. There were some 50 Negroes shot while in the water. I was shot at while standing in the water behind a log.

DANIEL H. (his x mark) RANKIN.

Sworn and subscribed to before me this 25th day of April, 1864.

WM. STANLEY,

Lieutenant and Assistant Provost-Marshal.

Statement of John F. Ray, Company B, Thirteenth Tennessee Cavalry:

I do hereby [certify] that I was at Fort Pillow, Tenn., on the 12th of the present month, when it was attacked by rebels under General Forrest. I was in the fort from the first. A continued fire was kept up until about 1 p.m., when the flag of truce came in from the Confederates. I saw the rebels massing and disposing their forces while the flag was under consideration. I also certify that at this time I saw some rebels come up even to the ditch beyond which our cannon were placed. I asked some of them why they came so close while the flag of truce was being canvassed. They only replied that they knew their business there. We threatened to fire if they came any nearer, when they jumped into the ditches outside out fort. Firing was resumed and lasted about one hour, when the rebels stormed our works. The Negroes ran. The white men also ran, both having thrown down their arms, but both were followed up closely by armed rebels, who shot down all indiscriminately. I was shot after I had surrendered, and while going down the bluff I saw 12 white soldiers and perhaps 30 Negroes shot down after surrender and while begging for mercy. I also certify that in one instance I saw a small Negro boy riding on a horse sitting behind a rebel lieutenant, when the lieutenant was ordered by a superior officer (I am not positive that it was General Chalmers) to take that "God damned Niger down and shoot him, or he would be shot himself." The order was obeyed, and the boy was killed.

Mound City, ill., April 23, 1864.

JOHN F. (his x mark) RAY.

Witness:

WILLIAM CLEARY,

Second Lieut. Co. B, Thirteenth Tennessee Cavalry.

Sworn and subscribed to before me this 23d day of April, 1864, at Mound City, Ill.

WM. STANLEY,

Lieutenant and Assistant Provost-Marshal.

Affidavit of Hardy N. Revelle:

I was in business at Fort Pillow previous the fight on Tuesday last; was engaged as a dry-goods clerk for Messrs. Harris & Co. Went into the fight at 6 0'clock on the mourning of Tuesday, the 12th of April. Remained outside of the Federal fortifications until about 8.30 a.m., acting as a sharpshooter. At this time we were all ordered within the fort. Lieutenant Barr was killed outside the fort; also lieutenant Wilson, latter of the Thirteenth Tennessee Cavalry.

It was not long after 9 0'clock that I took my position behind the fortifications and resumed the fight. I was standing not more than 10 paces from Major Booth when he fell, struck in the heart by a musket-bullet. It was but a few minutes past 9. He did not die immediately, but was borne from the field. At this time there was continued firing on both sides. Rebels were not using artillery; our troops were. The next thing I recollect is a flag of truce coming in, the bearer of which, General Forrest, of the rebel army, and some parties of his staff, demanded a surrender of the garrison. Major Bradford was then in command. Forrest did not come within the breast-works, but remained some 50 yards outside, and Major Bradford went out to meet him. They conferred in a southeasterly direction from what was known as old headquarters. Bradford is said to have replied that he would not surrender. Forrest told him if he did not there would not be any quarter shown. They were in conference about fifteen minutes, during which time there was a cessation of firing. Bradford asked for one hour's time in which to confer with the commander of the gun-boat. Forrest refused it, but I think there was a cessation of hostilities of nearly that length of time. The rebels were busily engaged in plundering our hastily deserted encampment outside the fortifications, as well as robbing some of the stores below the hill. They were also massing their troops and placing them in eligible positions while the flag of truce was being considered. It is my opinion that they could never have gained the positions had they not done so under that flag of truce. They already consumed seven or eight hours in attempting it, with no success.

At about 2.30 in the afternoon a large force of infantry came upon us from the ravine toward the east of where I stood. It seemed to come down Coal Creek. They charged upon our ranks. Another large force of rebel cavalry charged from the south of east, and another force from the northward. They mounted the breast-works at the first charge where I stood. We fired upon them while upon the breast-works. I remember firing two shots while the enemy were upon the walls. The Negro troops, frightened by the appearance of such numbers, and knowing they could no longer resist, made a break and ran down the hill, surrendering their arms as the rebels came down our side of the fortifications.

When we found there was no quarter to be shown, and that (white and black) we were to be butchered, we also gave up our arms and passed down the hill. It is stated that at this time Major Bradford put a white handkerchief on his sword-point and waved it in token of submission, but it was not heeded if he did. We were followed closely and fiercely by the advancing rebel forces, their fire never ceasing at all. Our men had given signals themselves that they surrendered, many of them throwing up their hands to show they were unarmed, and submitted to overwhelming odds. I was about half-way down the hill, partially secreted in a kind of ravine with Dr. Fitch, when I saw 2 men (white men) belonging to the Thirteenth Tennessee Cavalry standing behind a stump on which they had fixed a white handkerchief, their hands thrown up. They asked for quarter. When they stood on their feet they were exposed, and I saw them shot down by rebel soldiers and killed.

A captain of the rebel troops then came where we were and ordered all the Federals (white and black) to move up the hill or he would "shoot their God-damned brains out." I started up the hill with a number of others, in accordance with the order. I was surrendered with out men. While going up I saw white men fall on both sides of me, who were shot down by rebel soldiers who were stationed upon the brow of the hill. We were at the time marching directly toward the men who fired upon us. I do not know how many fell, but I remember of seeing 4 killed in this way. I also saw Negroes shot down with pistols in the hands of the rebels. One was killed at my side. I saw another Negro struck on the head with a saber by a rebel soldier. I suppose he was also killed. One more just in front of me was knocked down with the butt of a musket. We kept on up the hill. I expected each moment to meet my fate with the rest. At the top of the hill I met a man named Cutler, a citizen of Fort Pillow. He spoke to a rebel captain about me, and we then went under orders from the captain to one of the stores under the hill, where the captain got a pair of boots. This was about 4 p.m. on Tuesday.

The captain and Cutler and myself then left to fine General McCulloch's headquarters, where we were to report and be disposed of. The captain introduced me to a lieutenant and to a surgeon of the rebel army. The surgeon made me show him where goods could be found. The lieutenant got a saddle and bridle and some bits, and then we helped them carry them to where their horses were, outside of the fortifications. I also met Mr. Wedlin, a citizen, and he accompanied us. He helped the lieutenant to mount and pack his goods, and then he gave Wedlin and myself permission to depart, and instructed us as to the best means of escape.

I am positive that up to the time of surrender there had not been more than 50 men (black and white) killed and wounded on the Union side. Of these but about 20 had been among the killed. The balance of al killed and wounded on our side were killed and wounded after we had given undoubted evidence of a surrender, and contrary to all rules of warfare.

H.N. REVELLE.

Sworn to before me at Cairo, Ill., this 17th day of April, 1864.

JNO. H. MUNROE,

Captain and Assistant Adjutant-General.

Testimony of Sergt. Benjamin Robinson, Company D, Sixth U.S. Heavy Artillery:

I do hereby certify that I was in the battle at Fort Pillow on the 12th day of April, A.D. 1864, and that I was taken prisoner and while thus a prisoner was shot and wounded by a rebel soldier.

I also certify that I saw Sandy Sherman, of Company D, Sixth U.S. Heavy Artillery, murdered in cold blood while a prisoner in the hands of the rebels. I also saw George Wilborn shot down and killed after being taken prisoner.

Mound City, April 23, 1864.

BENJ. (his x mark) ROBINSON,

Sergeant Company D, U.S. Heavy Artillery.

Witness:

JOHN H. BAKER,

Captain Company B, Sixth U.S. Heavy Artillery (colored).

Sworn and subscribed to before me this 23d day of April, 1864, at Mound City, Ill.

WM. STANLEY,

Lieutenant and Assistant Provost-Marshal.

Statement of Mrs. Ann Jane Rufins:

I am the wife of Thomas Rufins, a member of the Thirteenth Tennessee Cavalry. Was at Fort Pillow on Tuesday, the 12th of April, A.D. 1864, and was removed to an island during the progress of the battle. Returned to Fort Pillow on Wednesday morning, the 13th of April, and saw the remains of a man lying upon the back, its arms stretched, with some planks under it. The man had to all appearances been nailed to the side of the house and then the building set on fire. I am satisfied that the body was that of Lieut. John C. Akerstrom, second Lieutenant Company A, Thirteenth Tennessee Cavalry, who was on duty as quartermaster of the post of Fort Pillow. I was well acquainted with Lieutenant Ackerstrom when living. After examining the body I walked around to a ditch where a large number of dead and wounded had been thrown and partially covered. I saw several places where the wounded had dug holes and attempted to get out, but had been unable to do so.

Cairo, April 18, 1864.

ANN JANE (her x mark) RUFINS.

Subscribed and sworn to before me this 18th day of April, 1864.

ISAAC M. TALMADGE,

Captain and District Provost-Marshal.

Statement of Daniel Stamps, Company E, Thirteenth Tennessee Cavalry:

I do hereby certify that I was at Fort Pillow, Tenn., on the 12th day of the present month, when it was attacked by the rebels under Forrest. I was ordered out as a sharpshooter, skirmished with the enemy about one hour, when I was called within the fort. We fired very deliberately while we were outside of the fort, and I saw a great many fall dead from the effects of our guns. I staid within the fort perhaps about one hour, when I was again taken as a sharpshooter to go down under the bluff to repulse the enemy, reported as coming down Coal Creek. We attained a good position where we could see the enemy very plainly, being ourselves secreted behind some logs. I kept up a steady fire all the time I was in this place, until the flag of truce came up, about 1 p.m., killing one of the enemy at nearly every shot. We were next ordered to cease firing. At that very moment the force of the enemy, which had been kept back by our sharpshooting, made an advance. I looked up and saw large bodies of infantry moving down Coal Creek re-enforcing those previously before us, and whose advance we had prevented. When the rebels had got a good position, where they could pick our men off as they came out of the fort, I saw them break ranks and get water out of the river and make every preparation for a fight, after which they resumed their line of battle. This they did while the flag of truce was being considered and all firing had ceased. The demand of the flag of truce having been refused, the firing was resumed, and I discharged my piece several times, bringing one rebel down at every shot; thus for about three-quarters of an hour keeping them from an advance. Afterward, when the Negroes had given way on the left, I saw the white soldiers coming down after them, saying the rebels were showing no quarter. I then threw down my gun and ran down with them, closely pursued by the enemy shooting down every man black and white. They said they had orders from Forrest to show no quarter, but to "kill the last God damned one of them." While I was standing at the bottom of the hill, I heard a rebel officer shout out an order of some kind to the men who had taken us, and saw a rebel soldier standing by me. I asked him what the officer had said. He repeated it to me again. It was, "kill the last damn one of them." The soldier replied to his officer that we had surrendered; that we were prisoners and must not be shot. The officer again replied, seeming crazy with rage that he had not been obeyed, "I tell you to kill the last God damned one of them." He then turned and galloped off. I also certify that I saw 2 men shot down while I was under the bluff. They fell nearly at my feet. They had their hands up; and had surrendered, and were begging for mercy. I also certify that I saw at least 25 Negroes shot down, within 10 or 20 paces from the place where I stood. They had also surrendered, and were begging for mercy.

I do also certify that on the ensuing morning I saw Negroes who were wounded, and had survived the night, shot and killed as fast as they could be found. One rebel threatened to kill me because I would not tell him where a poor Negro soldier was who had been wounded badly, but who had crawled off on his hands and knees and hidden behind a log. I was myself shot some two hours after I had surrendered.

Mound City. Ill., April 23, 1864.

DANIEL (his x mark) STAMPS.

Witness:

WILLIAM CLEARY,

Second Lieut. Co. B, 13th Tennessee Cavalry Vols.

Sworn and subscribed to before me this 25th day of April, 1864, at Mound City, Ill.

WM. STANLEY,

Lieutenant and Assistant Provost-Marshal.

Statement of James N. Taylor, Company E, Thirteenth Tennessee Cavalry:

I was at Fort Pillow, Tenn., on the 12th day of the present month when the place was attacked by rebels under Forrest. I was at first doing duty as a sharpshooter. After about two hours of that work I was ordered within the fort, and obeyed. About 1 p.m., while the flag of truce was under discussion, I plainly saw the enemy engaged in disposing their troops, plundering our camp, and stealing goods from the quartermaster's and other stores. They formed at the same time on two sides of our garrison, and placed their sharpshooters in our deserted barracks, After the order to surrender had been refused the enemy charged upon us, came over the walls in overwhelming force, and the Negroes first and then the whites afterward, threw down their arms and surrendered.

All then started to run down the bluff, closely pursued by and fired upon by the rebels. I was shot after I had surrendered, and while going down the bluff. I also saw them shoot down 12 colored soldiers, and that after they had surrendered. Some were on their knees with outstretched hands, begging for mercy. I also heard one of General Forrest's officers say, "kill them, God damn them; it is General Forrest's orders." I also saw on the next morning, the 13th of April, 1864, the rebels come upon the ground and kill all the wounded they could find. I saw them make two wounded Negroes stand upon their feet that they might see them fall again when shot; and shot they were.

Mound City, Ill., April 23, 1864.

JAMES N. (his x mark) TAYLOR.

Witness:

WILLIAM CLEARY,

Second Lieut. Company B, 13th Tennessee Cavalry.

Sworn and subscribed to before me this 25th day of April, 1864, at Mound City, Ill.

WM. STANLEY,

Lieutenant and Assistant Provost-Marshal.

Statement of William P. Walker, Company D, Thirteenth Tennessee Cavalry:

I hereby certify that I was at Fort Pillow, Tenn., on the 12th day of the present month, when it was attacked by the Confederates. I saw nothing more than has probably been related by a dozen others, until about the time of the panic and retreat down the bluff by both white and black Union troops. We were followed closely by the rebels and shot down after surrender as fast as they could find us. One of the rebels, after I had given him up my money as he ordered me, fired upon me twice, after I had surrendered and while I begged for my life. One ball struck me in the left eye. The rebels had almost ceased firing upon us when an officer came down and told them to "Shoot the last damned one of us," and "not to take one prisoner." He said it was orders of the general (I could not hear plainly, but I think it was Chalmers). Then the slaughter of the prisoners resumed. I saw some 6 white and 10 colored soldiers thus shot, long after they had surrendered, and while the Negroes were on their knees begging to be spared.

Mound City, Ill., April 23, A.D. 1864.

WM. P. (his x mark) WALKER.

Witness:

WILLIAM CLEARY,

Second Lieut. Company B, 13th Tennessee Cavalry.

Sworn and subscribed to before me this 25th day of April, 1864, at Mound City, Ill.

WM. STANLEY,

Lieutenant and Assistant Provost-Marshal.

Statement of Mrs. Rebecca Williams:

I am the wife of Wm. F. Williams, a private in the Thirteenth Tennessee Cavalry, Company D. I was at Fort Pillow on Wednesday morning after the fight of Tuesday, the 12th of April, 1864, and saw the body of a man which had the appearance of having been burned to death. It was pointed out to me as the body of Lieut. John C. Akerstrom, of the Thirteenth Cavalry. I know it was the corpse of a white man.

Cairo, April 18, 1864

REBECCA (her x mark) WILLIAMS.

Subscribed and sworn to before me this 18th day of April, 1864.

ISAAC M. TALMADGE,

Captain and District Provost-Marshal.

MOUND CITY, April 25, 1864.

Statement of Sergt. William A. Winn, Company B, Thirteenth Tennessee Cavalry Volunteers:

I was at Fort Pillow on Tuesday, the 12th of April, 1864, when the attack was made by General Forrest upon that place. At the firing of the first gun I hastened on board the gun-boat, as I had been wounded some time and could not fight. The first thing I saw afterward was the rebel sharpshooters on top of the hill and ours at quartermaster's department firing at each other, and the rebels were also firing at the gun-boat. The next thing I saw was a flag of truce come in, which was in waiting some half an hour. This was about 1 p.m., and as soon as it started back the enemy immediately started up the hill on the double-quick, not waiting for the flag of truce to return. as soon as they came close to the fort and had their sharpshooters distributed through our barracks (which were just outside the fort) they opened fire upon the garrison and then charged the works. Those troops that I saw came from the direction that the flag of truce did. I saw our men run down the bluff, the rebels after them shooting them down as fast as they came up with them. I saw 12 or 15 men shot down after they had surrendered, with their hands up begging for mercy. Next I saw them turn their cannon on us (the boat), and throw shells at the boat trying to sink her, but she steamed up the river out of range, leaving behind us a scene of cold blooded murder too cruel and barbarous for the human mind to express.

W.A. WINN.

Sworn and subscribed to before me this 25th day of April, 1864.

WM. STANLEY,

Lieutenant and Assistant Provost-Marshal.

HEADQUARTERS DISTRICT OF CAIRO,
May 4. 1864.

Hon. E.M. STANTON,

Secretary of War, Washington, D.C.

Sir: On April 28 I had the honor to transmit by the hand of Hon. B.F. Wade proofs concerning the affair at Fort Pillow.

On the 30th I also transmitted a duplicate thereof, intending one copy, if it pleased you, for the committee of which Mr. Wade is chairman.

I now, as therein promised, send additional proofs, since secured, to be added to those first sent.

Respectfully, your obedient servant,

M. BRAYMEN,

Brigadier-General of Volunteers.

Statement of Sandy Addison, private Company A, Sixth U.S. Heavy Artillery (colored):

I, Sandy Addison, private Company A, sixth U.S. Artillery (colored), would on oath state the following:

I was in the battle fought at Fort Pillow, Tenn., on the 12th day of April, A.D. 1864, and that I was taken prisoner about 5 p.m. same day. After the fort had been carried by the enemy the U.S. troops took shelter under the bluff of the hill, the officers all being killed or wounded. The white flag was raised by one of the colored men, but they kept firing upon us. I do not know how many, but a great many were killed under the white flag. I was taken over 2 miles, and camped for the night. There were several other prisoners with us. The surgeon dressed their wounds. He sent 3 colored man back to the river under the flag of truce. After they had got a little way off the rebels shot them down while they were going back to the boat; afterward they shot a man (he being wounded he could not go fast enough), and made some plantation hands bury him.

I was prisoner five days, and made my escape.

SANDY (his x mark) ADDISON.

Sworn to and subscribed before me this 30th day of April, 1864, at Fort Pickering, Memphis, Tenn.

MALCOLM F. SMITH,

First Lieut. and Adjt. 6th U.S. Heavy Artillery (colored).

Statement of Wilbur H. Gaylord, first sergeant Company B, Sixth U.S. Heavy Artillery (colored):

I was in the battle fought at Fort Pillow on the 12th day of April, A.D. 1864. The engagement commenced about 6.30 a.m. I was stationed about 20 rods outside the fort, with 20 men, and a southwest direction (this was about 6.30 a.m.), with orders from Maj. L.F. Booth to hold the position as long as possible without being captured. I staid there with the men about one hour. While there the rebels came within 30 rods, and tried to steal horses. They got two horses, and at the same time stuck a rebel flag on the fortifications. While I held this position the white men (Thirteenth Tennessee Cavalry) on my right retreated to the fort. About ten minutes after this I went with my men to the fort. While going into the fort I saw Lieutenant Barr, Thirteenth Tennessee Cavalry, shot down by my side. He was shot through the head. He fell outside the fortifications about 6 feet. Ten minutes after getting into the fort Maj. L.F. Booth was shot at port-hole no. 2, while standing directly in the rear of the gun; was shot directly through the heart; expired instantly. I carried him to the bank of the river. As soon as I returned Captain Epenter, Company A, was wounded in the head while standing at port hole No. 4. He immediately went to the hospital, which was below the riverbank, about half way down I should think

Ten men were killed before a flag of truce came in, which was about 12 m. Five men, who were all dressed alike came with the flag from the rebels, and Major Bradford, of the Thirteenth Tennessee Cavalry, who had now assumed command, asked for one hour's time to consider, on the conclusion of which he returned a decided refusal. The fire on both sides now commenced and was kept up about half an hour with great fury, when the rebels charged over the works. (I should have said that General Forrest came with the flag.) The enemy was checked and held for a few minutes. As soon as they were fairly on the works I was wounded with a musket-ball through the right ankle. I should think that 200 rebels passed over the works and passed by me while I lay there. when one rebel noticed that I was alive, he shot at me again and missed me. I told him I was wounded and that I would surrender, when a Texas ranger stepped up and took me prisoner. Just at this time I saw them shoot down 3 black men who were begging for their lives, and who had surrendered. The rebels now helped me through port-hole No. 4. The ranger who took me captured a colored soldier whom he sent with me; he also sent a guard. They took me to picket-post No. 2 There I was put into an ambulance and taken to a farm-house with one of their dead, who was a chaplain. There I was made to lie out doors all night on account of the house being filled with their wounded. I bandaged my own wound with my drawers, and a colored man brought water and set by me so that I could keep my foot wet.

Next morning Colonel McCulloch came there and sent a squad of men, having pressed all the conveyances he could find to take away his own wounded. Not finding sufficient, nor having Negroes enough they made stretchers of blankets. They could not carry me, and so left me at the farm-house. The man's name was Stone. He got me into the house, and into bed. He and his wife were very kind to me.

While Colonel McCulloch was there he told me Memphis, Tenn., was probably in the hands of the rebels. The rear guard of the rebels left there Wednesday about 5 p.m. The rebels took a young man whose father lived near here, and who had been wounded in the fight, to the woods and shot three more shots into his back and into his head and left him until Friday morning, when the citizens took him in. They brought him to the house where I was and then carried us both to Fort Pillow in a cart that they fixed up for the occasion, in hopes of getting us on board of a gun-boat. Upon our arrival there, a gun-boat lay on the opposite bank, but we could not hail her. We laid on the bank. They took the young man back to a house three-fourths of a mile, but I would not go back. I laid there until a gun-boat, the Silver Cloud took me off about 2 a.m. Saturday. They treated me with the utmost kindness on board the boat.

Fort Pickering, Tenn., April 28, 1864.

WILBUR H. GAYLORD,

First Sergt. Co. B, 6th U.S. Heavy Artillery (colored), 1st Batt.

Sworn to and subscribed before me this 30th day of April, 1864,

at Fort Pickering, Memphis, Tenn.

MALCOLM F. SMITH,

First Lieut. and Adjt. 6th U.S. Heavy Artillery (colored).

Statement of Frank Hogan, Corporal Company A, Sixth U.S. Heavy Artillery (colored).

I, Frank Hogan, corporal in Company A, of the sixth Regiment U.S. Heavy Artillery (colored), would on oath state the following:

That I was in the battle fought at Fort Pillow, Tenn., on the 12th day of April, A.D. 1864; and that I was taken prisoner by the enemy, and I saw Captain Carson and heard some of the enemy ask him if he belonged to a Niger regiment. He told them he did. They now asked him how he came here. He told them he was detailed there. Then they told him they would give him a detail, and immediately shot him dead, after being a prisoner without arms. I also saw 2 Lieutenants, whose names I did not know, but who belonged to the Thirteenth Tennessee Cavalry. I also saw them kill 3 sick men lying helpless in their tents. I saw them make our men (colored) pull the artillery, whipping them at the same time in a most shameful manner. I also saw them bury 1 of our men alive, being only wounded. I heard Colonel McCulloch, C.S. Army, ask his adjutant how many men were killed and wounded. The adjutant told him he had a list of 300, and that all reports were not in yet. colonel McCulloch was commanding a brigade. I also heard a captain, C.S. Army, tell Colonel McCulloch, C.S. Army, that 10 men were killed out of his own company.

FRANK (his x mark) HOGAN.

Sworn to and subscribed before me this 30th day of April, 1864, at
Fort Pickering, Memphis, Tenn.
MALCOLM F. SMITH,
First Lieut. and Adjt. 6th U.S. Heavy Artillery (colored).

Statement of George Huston private of Company B, Sixth Regiment U.S. Heavy Artillery (colored):

I, George Huston, private of Company B, sixth Regiment U.S. Heavy Artillery, would on oath state the following:

That I was in the battle fought at Fort Pillow on the 12th day of April, A.D. 1864, and that the fort was carried by the enemy about 3 p.m. of the 12th of April. The remaining portion of our troops fled from the fort and took refuge under the river bank, when Corpl. Jerry Stewart and Sergt. Manuel Underwood raised a white flag, but the enemy paid no attention to it at all. A rebel officer rode up to the bank and said that General Forrest ordered every damned Niger to be shot down. So the enemy kept on firing on our defenseless men, and killed a great many of them. I heard firing all night, but I hid myself under the bank of the river till the gun-boat no. 28 came to my relief.

GEORGE (his x mark) HUSTON.

Sworn and subscribed to before me this 30th day of April, 1864, at
Fort Pickering, Memphis, Tenn.
MALCOLM F. SMITH,
First Lieut. and Adjt. 6th U.S. Heavy Artillery (colored).

Statement of Jerry Stewart, corporal Company A, Sixth U.S. Heavy Artillery (colored):

I, Jerry Stewart, corporal Company A, Sixth U.S. Heavy Artillery (colored), would on oath state the following:

That I was in the battle fought at Fort Pillow, Tenn., on the 12th day of April, A.D. 1864, and I was taken prisoner about 4 p.m. of the same day by the Confederates. After the enemy had carried the works I saw them shoot about 100 colored men down when they were without arms. They shot 1 down by my side while we were going up the hill, and he fell against me. They shot at me several times. but I did not get wounded. I saw a sutler (A. Alexander) cruelly murdered by the rebels [sic]. They asked him first where he belonged. He told them he was a sutler. They then told him he was no better than the rest, and they shot him and buried him with some colored men. I heard a lieutenant in the Confederate army say that a Federal tried to get away, and he put five balls through him. I saw Capt. Charles J. Epenter, Lieut. P. Bishoff, First Sergt. John Thompson, of Company A, Sixth Regiment U.S. Heavy Artillery (colored), taken prisoners. Lieut. D. Hubank [J.J. Eubank?] told me to tell him if there were any Niger officers taken prisoners, and to point them out to him. I told him I did not know of any. A private soldier of the Confederate army told me that all the colored boys that could escape had best to do so by all means, for General Forrest was going to burn or whip them to death after they got farther south.

JERRY (his x mark) STEWART,
First Lieut. and Adjt. 6th U.S. colored Heavy Artillery.

Statement of Henry F. Weaver, first sergeant Company C, Sixth U.S. Heavy Artillery (colored), of the battle at Fort Pillow, Tenn., on the 12th day of April, 1864:

I called the roll of my company soon after daylight, and had gone to the bank of the river, and was there talking to Second Lieutenant T. W. McClure, of my company, and had not been there long when we heard an uncommon noise and commotion around headquarters, and soon the cry that the rebels were coming. we had the company fall in as soon as possible, when we were ordered to take possession of two 10-pounder Parrott guns, and soon another order to take them inside the works, which was done immediately and put in battery on the south end of the works, Lieutenant McClure taking command of the right gun and giving me the left gun, for which I had to build a platform before it could be used to any effect; but the platform was soon built and the gun in position, and I was firing at the advancing enemy as they came in sight. In the mean time Company B, Thirteenth Tennessee Cavalry, had left their camp on a hill in front of our main fort and came rushing back in disorder, leaving their horses and all their camp equipage behind.

The rebels soon commenced running off the horses under brisk fire of musketry and a section of artillery of Company D, Second U.S. Light Artillery (colored), commanded by First Lieutenant Hunter. Still farther to the left was a section of light artillery, manned by Company A, Sixth U.S. Heavy Artillery, under the command of Captain Epenter and Lieutenant Bishoff. By this time (8 o' clock) the enemy's sharpshooters had commenced a brisk fire on the fort, which was kept up with little intermission until about 2 o' clock, when the flag of truce was sent in demanding surrender. Early in the action Lieutenant Hill, Company C, Sixth U.S. and post adjutant, was killed while outside the fort setting fire to the quarters of the Thirteenth Cavalry, and it was not long before Major Booth, of the Sixth U.S., and commander of the post, was killed, falling near the trail of my gun, and was carried away. The command was devolved upon Major Bradford, of the Thirteenth Tennessee Cavalry. About noon the rebels commenced receiving reinforcements, and soon advanced close up to the fort, getting into the houses of the cavalry and some rifle-pits we had made a few days before, and which proved of more use to them than to us, and kept up such a brisk fire that it was almost impossible to work the guns. The cannoneers were all killed or wounded at my place except one or two, and also Lieutenant Hunter's gun, and my ammunition was almost gone; and I will here state that not more than one in five of the shells burst, owing to poor fuses. It was near 2 o' clock when a flag of truce was seen advancing, and the firing ceased on both sides, and an officer was sent by Major Bradford to see what was wanted. He soon returned with a demand for our surrender, stating that our brave defense had entitled us to be treated as prisoners of war; but if we did not surrender they should charge our works, and we would have to take the consequences. All this time the rebels took advantage of the truce and moved up close under our works, and took their positions ready for a charge. The demand to surrender was refused, and up to this time but a few had been killed but a good many wounded; but now the charge came, and as they came they gave their usual yell, and the Thirteenth Cavalry fled for the banks of the river. When the cavalry commenced to break our colored men wavered, and the rebels had by this time succeeded in entering the fort. Lieutenant Van Horn begged and ordered them to stop, but each one sought safety in flight, as the rebels had commenced an indiscriminate slaughter of the black soldiers, and, as far as I could see, every one was shot down as fast as the rebels could shoot their guns and revolvers. Some were shot down so close to me that they would nearly fall on me. I surrendered, the rebel remarking that they did not shoot white men, but wanted to know what in hell I was fighting with the damned Niger for. I soon got away from him, for he was to intent on murder in mind; but had gone but a few steps when another rebel met me and demanded my greenbacks, and after they robbing me of everything but my clothes he left me as not worthy of his further notice.

I then went down the river to the quartermaster's house, where I found Lieutenant Van Horn. We staid there about ten minutes, when a rebel came in and again demanded our surrender. I told him I had done so twice already. He then ordered us to follow him. We did, going up into town and into a store, where he commenced to pillage and I to get on some citizens clothing, which I soon did, and got out of the store. I now missed Lieutenant Van Horn, and did not see him again until the next Sunday, when I found he had escaped and got back to Fort Pickering before me. Companies B and D were outside the fort in rifle-pits until the enemy received his reinforcements, when they retired inside of the fort. Major Booth, from the time he took command of the post at Fort Pillow, was strengthening the same by throwing up rifle-pits, building platforms, and making embrasures in the fort for the purpose of working his guns. I succeeded in making my escape by getting citizen's clothing and playing off as a rebel. I then hid myself under the bank of the river until a tug-boat came along, which I boarded.

HENRY F. WEAVER,

Company C, Sixth U.S. Heavy Artillary (colored).

Sworn to and subscribed before me this 29th day of April, 1864, at

Fort Pickering, Memphis, Tenn.

MALCOLM F. WEAVER,

First Lieut. and Adjt. sixth U.S. Heavy Artillery (colored).

Statement of Jacob Wilson, private of Company B, Sixth U.S. Heavy Artillery (colored):

I, Jacob Wilson, a private of Company B, Sixth U.S. Heavy Artillery, would on oath state the following:

That I was in the battle fought at Fort Pillow on the 12th day of April, A.D. 1864, and after seven hours' hard fighting we were overpowered and driven down the bank from the fort. At that time, the officers all being wounded, the men threw down their arms and were taken prisoners by the enemy. I saw Sergt. William Morgan, Private Reuben Jones, Private William Lincoln, Private Samuel Tangesley, and Private Charles Cross, of Company B, Sixth U.S. Heavy Artillery (colored), and many others of the regiment, shot by the rebels after they had taken us prisoners.

JACOB (his x mark) WILSON,

Sworn to and subscribed to before me this 29th day of April, 1864,

at Fort Pickering, Tenn.

MALCOLM F. SMITH,

First Lieut. and Adjt. Sixth U.S. Heavy Artillery (colored).

Report of Lieut. Col. Thomas H. Harris, Assistant Adjutant-General,

U.S. Army, of the garrison at Fort Pillow, etc."'

HEADQUARTERS SIXTEENTH ARMY CORPS,

Memphis, Tenn., April 26, 1864.

Sir: I wish to state that one section of Company D, Second U.S. Light Artillery (colored), 1 commissioned officer and 40 men, were sent to Fort Pillow about February 15, as part of the garrison.

The garrison at Fort Pillow, by last reports received, consisted of the First Battalion, Sixth U.S. Heavy Artillery (colored), 8 commissioned officers and 213 enlisted men; one section Company D, Second U.S. Light Artillery (colored), 1 commissioned officer and 40 men; First Battalion, Thirteenth Tennessee Cavalry, Maj. W.F. Bradford, 10 commissioned officers and 285 enlisted men. Total white troops, 295; total colored troops, 262; grand total, 557. six field pieces, consisting of two 6-pounders, two 12 pounder howitzers, and two 10-pounder Parrotts.

T.H. HARRIS,

Lieutenant-Colonel and Assistant Adjutant-General.

13TH TENNESSEE CAVALRY, ADJUTANT MACK J.LEAMING'S

REPORT OF THE CAPTURE OF FORT PILLOW

Report of Lieut. Mack J. Leaming, Adjutant Thirteenth Tennessee Cavalry, to Hon. E.M. STANTON, Secretary of War, on the capture of Fort Pillow.

ADJUTANT-GENERAL'S OFFICE, STATE OF TENNESSEE,
Nashville, Tenn., January 17, 1865.

Sir: I have the honor to acknowledge the receipt of your communication of the 31st ultimo, and , in accordance with the direction therein contained, to make the following report of the battle of Fort Pillow:

On the 12th day of April, 1864, the Federal forces stationed at Fort Pillow, Tenn., consisted of one battalion of the Sixth U.S. Heavy Artillery (colored troops), one battery Second U.S. Light Artillery (colored troops), and the Thirteenth Regiment West Tennessee Volunteer Cavalry, which was then recruiting, having four companies mustered into the U.S. service and the fifth company ready for muster. The men composing this company had been enlisted by Capt. John L. Poston, and repeated applications had been made to have them mustered into the U.S. service, but no mustering officer could be sent for that purpose. Our entire garrison numbered some 550 effective men, with six pieces of artillery, the whole under command of Maj. L.F. Booth, of the Sixth U.S. Heavy Artillery (colored troops). In addition to this force the U.S. gun-boat New Era, Captain Marshall, was stationed off Fort Pillow and participated in the engagement, but owing to high bluffs, and in consequence of the long range she was obliged to take with her guns but little assistance was rendered the garrison from this quarter.

At 5.30 o'clock on the morning of the 12th of April, 1864, our pickets were attacked and driven in by the advance of the enemy, under command of General Forrest. Our garrison immediately opened fire on the advancing rebels from our artillery at the fort, while Companies D and E, of the Thirteenth West Tennessee Cavalry, were deployed as skirmishers, which duty they performed until about 8 a.m., when they were compelled to retire to the fort after considerable loss, in which Lieutenant Barr, of company D, was killed.

The firing continued without cessation, principally from behind logs, stumps, and under cover of thick underbrush and from high knolls, until about 9 a.m., when the rebels made a general assault on our works, which was successfully repulsed with severe loss to them and but slight loss to our garrison. We, however, suffered pretty severely in the loss of commissioned officers by the unerring aim of the rebel sharpshooters, and among this loss I have to record the name of our post commander, Maj. L.F. Booth, who was killed almost instantly by a musket-ball through the breast.

Maj. W.F. Bradford, of the Thirteenth West Tennessee Volunteer Cavalry, being the next ranking officer, then assumed command of the garrison and directed the remainder of our operations.

At about 11 a.m. the rebels made a second determined assault on our works. In this attempt they were again successfully repulsed with severe loss. The enemy succeeded, however, in obtaining possession of two rows of barracks running parallel to the south side of the fort and distant about 150 yards. The barracks had previously been ordered to be destroyed, but after severe loss on our part in the attempt to execute the order our men were compelled to retire without accomplishing the desired end, save only to the row nearest to the fort. From these barracks the enemy kept up a murderous fire on our men, despite all our efforts to dislodge him.

Owing to the close proximity of these buildings to the fort, and to the fact that they were on considerably lower ground, our artillery could not be sufficiently depressed to destroy them, or even render them untenable for the enemy. Musketry and artillery firing continued, however, on both sides with great energy, and although our garrison was almost completely surrounded, all attempts of the enemy to carry our works by assault were successfully repulsed, not-withstanding his great superiority in numbers.

At 3.30 p.m. firing suddenly ceased in consequence of the appearance of a white flag displayed by the enemy. The party bearing the flag was halted about 150 yards from the fort, when we were informed by one of the party that they had a communication from General Forrest to the commanding officer of the U.S. forces at Fort Pillow. I was ordered out, accompanied by Captain Bradford and Young, to receive this communication, which I took back to the fort while the party bearing the same remained for an answer. As nearly as I can remember the communication was as follows:

HEADQUARTERS CONFEDERATE CAVALRY,
Near Fort Pillow, Tenn., April 12, 1864.

Maj. L.F. Booth,
Commanding U.S. Forces at Fort Pillow:
MAJOR: Your gallant defense of Fort Pillow has entitled you to the treatment of brave men. I now demand the unconditional surrender of your forces, at the same time assuring you that you will be treated as prisoners of war. I have received a new supply of ammunition and can take your works by assault, and if compelled to do so you must take the consequences.
Very respectfully, your obedient servant,
N.B. FORREST,
Major-General, Commanding Confederate Cavalry.

To this communication I was ordered to make the following reply, which I placed in a sealed envelope, addressed to Major-General Forrest, and delivered to the party in waiting:

HEADQUARTERS U.S. FORCES,
Fort Pillow, Tenn., April 12, 1864.
Maj. Gen. N.B. FORREST,
Commanding Confederate Cavalry:
General: Yours of this instant is received, and in reply I have to ask one hour for consultation and consideration with my officers and the officers of the gun-boat.
Very respectfully, your obedient servant,
L.F. BOOTH,

Major, Commanding U.S. Forces.
Desiring to conceal from the enemy the fact of the death of Major Booth and cause him to believe that he was still in command, it was deemed not only proper but advisable that I append his name to the communication.

I again returned to the fort, where I had been but a few minutes when the party bearing the white flag again made its appearance with a second communication, and I was again sent out to meet the communication, another officer galloped up and said, "That gives you twenty minutes to surrender; I am General Forrest." This I took back to the fort, the party remaining as before for an answer. It read as follows:

HEADQUARTERS CONFEDERATE CAVALRY,
Near Fort Pillow, April 12, 1864.

Maj. L.F. Booth,
Commanding U.S. Forces at Fort Pillow:
Major: I do not demand the surrender of the gun-boat; twenty minutes will be given you to take your men outside the fort and surrender. If in that time this demand is not complied with I will immediately proceed to assault your works, and you must take the consequences.
Very respectfully, your obedient servant,
N.B. FORREST,
Major-General. C.S. Army.

After a short consultation with the officers of the garrison, it was unanimously voted not to surrender. In accordance with this decision I was ordered to write and deliver to the party in waiting the following communication:

HEADQUARTERS U.S. FORCES,
Fort Pillow, Tenn., April 12, 1864.
Maj. Gen. N.B. Forrest,
Commanding Confederate Cavalry:
General: I will not surrender.
Very respectfully, your obedient servant,
L.F. BOOTH,
Commanding U.S. Forces, Fort Pillow.
This I delivered to General Forrest in person, who broke open the envelope in my presence and after a hasty persual of its contents re-folded it, when we simply saluted and each went our way.
During the cessation of the firing on both sides, in consequence of the flag of truce offered by the enemy, and while the attention of both officers and men was naturally directed to the south side of the fort where the communications were being received and answered, Forrest had resorted to means the most foul and infamous ever adopted in the most barbarous ages of the world for the accomplishment of his design. Here he took occasion to move his troops, partially under cover of a ravine and thick under-brush, into the very position he had been fighting to obtain throughout the entire en-gagement, up to 3.30 p.m. Consequently, when the final decision of the garrison had been made known, the rebel charge was immediately sounded; when, as if rising from out of the earth on the center and north side, within 20 yards of our works, the rebels received our first fire, wavered, rallied again and finally succeeded in breaking our lines, and in thus gaining possession of the fort. At this juncture, one company of the Sixth U.S. Heavy Artillery, colored troops, rushed down the bluff, at the summit of which were our works, and many of them jumped into the river, throwing away their arms as they fled.

Seeing that through a gross violation of the rules of civilized warfare the enemy had now gained possession of our works, and in consequence that it would be useless to offer further resistance, our men threw down their arms and surrendered. For a moment the fire seemed to slacken. The scene which followed, however, beggars all description. The enemy carried our works at about 4 p.m., and from that time until dark, and at intervals throughout the night, our men were shot down without mercy and almost without regard to color. This horrid work of butchery did not cease even with the night of murder, but was renewed again the next morning, when numbers of our wounded were basely murdered after a long night of pain and suffering on the field where they had fought so bravely.

Of this display of Southern Chivalry, of this wholesale butchery of brave men, white as well as black, after they had surrendered, and of the innumerable barbarities committed by the rebels on our sick in the hospitals and the bodies of our dead, I do not deem it necessary further to speak, inasmuch as the committee on the conduct of the War was made a full and accurate report of the same, in which the barbarities practiced by the rebels at Fort Pillow are shown to have been horrid in the extreme, and fully confirming even the most seemingly exaggerated statements.

The fate of Maj. William F. Bradford, for a while involved in some degree of doubt and obscurity, seems now to be clearly established. Subsequent events show beyond a reasonable doubt that he was brutally murdered the first night of his capture.

Of the commissioned officers of the Thirteenth West Tennessee Volunteer Cavalry (now the Fourteenth Regiment), all were killed save First Lieutenant Nicholas D. Logan, of C Company, who died in prison at Macon, Ga., on the 9th June, 1864, and myself, the adjutant of the regiment.

The rebels were very bitter against these loyal Tennesseans, terming them "home made Yankees," and declaring they would give them no better treatment than they dealt out to the Negro troops with whom they were fighting.

At about 10 a.m. the day following the capture of the fort, while the U.S. gun-boat no. 28 from Memphis was shelling the enemy, who at the same time was engaged in murdering our wounded, Forrest sent a flag of truce to the commander granting him from that time until 5 p.m. to bury our dead and remove the few surviving wounded, he having no means of attending to them. This proposal was accepted, and under it myself with some 59 others, all that were left of the wounded, were carried on board the transport Platte Valley and taken to Mound City, Ill., where we received good care and treatment in the U.S. general hospital at that place.

But one commissioned officer of the garrison besides myself lived to get there, and he (Lieutenant Porter) died soon afterward from the effect of his wound.

Of the number, white and black, actually murdered after the surrender I cannot say positively; however, from my own observation, as well as from prisoners who were captured at Fort Pillow and afterward made their escape, I cannot estimate that number at anything less than 300.

From what I could learn at the time of the fight, as well as from escaped prisoners since then, relative to the Confederate loss in the attack and capture of Fort Pillow, I am confident that 500 men in killed and wounded would not be an overestimate. The Confederate forces engaged, as nearly as I could ascertain, numbered some 7,000 men, under command of General Forrest, Chalmers, and McCulloch.

The bravery of our troops in the defense of Fort Pillow, I think, cannot be questioned. Many of the men, and particularly the colored soldiers, had never before been under fire; yet every man did his duty with a courage and determined resolution, seldom if ever surpassed in similar engagements.

Had Forrest not violated the rules of civilized warfare in taking advantage of the flag of truce in the manner I have mentioned in another part of this report, I am confident we could have held the fort against all his assaults during the day, when, if we had been properly supported during the night by the Major-General commanding at Memphis, a glorious victory to the Union cause would have been the result of the next day's operations.

In conclusion, it may not be altogether improper to state that I was one of the number wounded, at first considered mortally, after the surrender; and but for the aid soon afterward extended to me by a Confederate Captain, who was a member of an order to which I belong (Free Masonry), I would in all probability have shared the fate of many of my comrades who were murdered after having been wounded. This captain had me carried into a small shanty, where he gave me some brandy and water. He was soon ordered to his company, and I was carried by the rebels into the barracks which they had occupied during the most of the engagement. Here had been collected a great number of our wounded, some of whom had already died.

Early the next morning these barracks were set on fire by order of a rebel officer. who had been informed that they contained Federal wounded. I was rendered entirely helpless from the nature of my wound, the ball having entered my right side, and ranging downward, grazed my lung, and deeply embedded itself in my hip (where it still remains) out of easy reach of surgical instruments. In this condition I had almost given up hope of being saved from a horrible death, when one of my own men, who was less severely wounded than myself, succeeded in drawing me out of the building, which the flames were then rapidly consuming.

As to the course our Government should pursue in regard to the outrages perpetrated by the rebels on this as well as on a number of occasions during the existing rebellion. I have only to express my method of preventing recurrence of the fiendish barbarities practiced on the defenders of our flag at Fort Pillow.

I am. sir, very respectfully, your obedient servant,

MACK J. LEAMING,

Lieut. and Adjt. 14th Tennessee Vol. Cav., late 13th Regt.

RECOMMENDATION TO PRESIDENT LINCOLN CONCERNING THE BATTLE AT FORT PILLOW

War Department, Washington City, May 5, 1864.

His Excellency the PRESIDENT OF THE UNITED STATES:

Sir: Upon the question propounded to my consideration by you I have the honor to submit the following opinion:

First. That of the rebel officers now held as prisoners by the United States there should be selected by lot a number equal to the number of persons ascertained to have been massacred at Fort Pillow, who shall immediately be placed in close confinement as hostages to await such further action as may be determined.

Second. That Generals Forrest and Chalmers and all officers and men known, or who may hereafter be ascertained, to have been concerned in the massacre at Fort Pillow be excluded by the President's special order from the benefit of his amnesty, and also that they, by his order, be exempted from privilege of exchange or other rights as prisoners of war, and shall, if they fall into our hands, be subjected to trial and such punishment as may be awarded for their barbarous and inhuman violation of the laws of war toward the officers and soldiers of the United States at Fort Pillow.

Third. That the rebel authorities at Richmond be notified that the prisoners so selected are held as hostages for the delivery up of Generals Forrest and Chalmers and those concerned in the massacre at Fort Pillow, or to answer in their stead, and in case of their non-delivery within a reasonable time, to be specified in the notice, such measures will be taken in reference to the hostages, by way of retribution justice for the massacre of Fort Pillow, as are justified by the laws of civilized warfare.

Fourth. That after the lapse of a reasonable time for the delivery up of Chalmers, Forrest, and those concerned in the massacre the President proceed to take against the hostages above selected such measures as may, under the state of things then existing, be essential for the protection of Union soldiers from savage barbarities as were practiced at Fort Pillow and to compel the rebels to observe the laws of civilized warfare.

Fifth. That the practice of releasing without exchange of equivalent rebel prisoners taken in battle be discontinued, and no such immunity be extended to rebels while our prisoners are undergoing ferocious barbarity or the more terrible death of starvation.

Lincoln chose to wait until he had the results of the wilderness campaign before making a decision as to what course should be taken against the Confederacy for the atrocities commited at Fort Pillow. After the Wilderness campaign the Fort Pillow affair seemed to lose steam, and was slowly forgotten due to the upcoming presidential campaign. However, the Union soldier did not forget Fort Pillow.

REPORTS FROM MAJOR GENERAL WASHBURN, U.S. ARMY TRANSMITTING CORRESPONDENCE WITH MAJOR GENERAL STEPHEN D. LEE AND MAJOR GENERAL NATHAN B. FORREST, C.S. ARMY

After Fort Pillow, black soldiers and white soldiers fighting beside black soldiers believed that the Confederate Army had raised the "Black Flag" and taken a "No Quarter" stance against them. This belief resulted in many instances of Union soldiers taking revenge upon the southern soldiers when they could. At the battle of Resaca in May 1864, the 105th Illinois captured a Confederate battery. From underneath one of the gun carriages a big, red-haired man with no shirt fearfully emerged. He wore a tattoo on one arm that read "Fort Pillow." His captors read it. He was bayoneted and shot instantly. Another regiment in Sherman's army was reported to have killed twenty-three rebel prisoners, first asking them if they remembered Fort Pillow. The Wisconsin soldier who recorded this incident claimed flatly, "When there is no officer with us, we take no prisoners." They would revenge their brother soldiers. Union soldiers regarded the Fort Pillow incident as proof that, as one put it, the rebels were as savage as Indians. At Resaca and elsewhere they retaliated.

The rumors of Black soldiers taking an oath to show the Confederate soldiers no quarter in order to avenge Fort Pillow prompted Confederate Major General Nathan B. Forrest to begin a series of correspondence with Major General Cadwaller C. Washburn, U.S. Army, who had recently replaced Major General Hurlbut by orders of General Grant. This series also includes correspondence with Confederate Major General Stephen D. Lee, Confederate secretary of war J.A. Seddon, and a final letter from Confederate President Jefferson Davis.

HEADQUARTERS FORREST'S CAVALRY,
In the Field, June 14, 1864.
[Maj. Gen. C.C. Washburn:]
General: I have the honor herewith to inclose copy of the letter received from Brigadier-General Buford, commanding U.S. forces at Helena, Ark., addressed to Col. E.W. Rucker, commanding Sixth Brigade of this command; also a letter from myself to General Buford, which I respectfully request you to read and forward to him.

There is a matter also to which I desire to call to your attention, which until now I have not thought proper to make the subject of a communication. Recent events render it necessary, in fact demand it.

It has been reported to me that all the negro troops stationed in Memphis took an oath on their knees, in presence of Major-General Hurlbut and other officers of your army, to avenge Fort Pillow, and that they would show my troops no quarter. Again, I have it from indisputable authority that the troops under Brigadier-General Sturgis, on their recent march from Memphis, publicly and in various places proclaimed that no quarter would be shown my men. As his troops were moved into action on the 11th [10th] the officers commanding exhorted their men to remember Fort Pillow, and a large majority of the prisoners we have captured from that command have voluntarily stated that they expected us to murder them; otherwise they would have surrendered in a body rather than taken to the bush after being run down and exhausted. The recent battle of Tishomingo Creek was far more bloody than it would otherwise have been but for the fact that your men evidently expected to be slaughtered when captured, and both sides acted as though neither felt safe in surrendering, even when further resistance was useless. The prisoners captured by us say they felt condemned by the announcement, &c.,[and] of their own commanders, and expected no quarter.

In all my operations since the war began I have conducted the war on civilized principals, and desire still to do so, but it is due to my command that they should know the position they occupy and the policy you intend to pursue. I therefor respectfully ask whether my men now in your hands are treated as other Confederate prisoners; also, the course intended to be pursued in regard to those who may hereafter fall into your hands.

I have in my possession quite a number of wounded officers and men of Sturgis' command, all of whom have been treated as well as we are able to treat them, and are mostly in charge of a surgeon left at Ripley by General Sturgis to look after the wounded. Some of them are to severely wounded to be removed at present. I am willing to exchange them for any men of my command you may have, and as soon as they are able to be removed will give them safe escort through my lines in charge of the surgeon left with them. I made such an arrangment with Major-General Hurlbut when he was in command at Memphis, and am willing to renew it, provided it is desired, as it would be better than subject them to the long and fatiguing trip necessary to a regular exchange at City Point, Va.

I am, very respectfully, your most obedient servant,

N.B. Forrest,

Major-General.

HEADQUARTERS DISTRICT OF WEST TENNESSEE,
Memphis, Tenn., June 17, 1864.
Maj. Gen. S.D. Lee,
Commanding Confederate Forces, near Tupelo, Miss.:

GENERAL: When I heard that the forces of Brigadier-General Sturgis had been driven back and a portion of them probably captured, I felt considerable solicitude for the fate of the two colored regiments that formed a part of the command, until I was informed that the Confederate forces were commanded by you. When I learned that, I became satisfied that no atrocities would be committed upon these troops, but that they would receive the treatment which humanity as well as their gallant conduct demanded.

I regret to say thet the hope that I entertained has been dispelled by facts which have recently come to my knowledge. From statements that have been made to me by colored soldiers who were eyewitnesses, it would seem that the massacre of Fort Pillow had been reproduced at the late affair at Brice's Cross-Roads. The details of the atrocities there committed I will not trouble you with. If true and not disavowed they must lead to consequences hereafter fearfule to contemplate.

It is best that we should now have a fair understanding upon the question of the treatment of this class of soldiers. If it is contemplated by the Confederate Government to murder all colored troops that may by chance of war fall into their hands, as was the case at Fort Pillow, it is but fair that it should be freely and frankly avowed.

Within the last six weeks I have on two occasions sent colored troops into the field from this point. In the expectation that the Confederate Government would disavow the action of the commanding general at the Fort Pillow massacre I have forborne to issue any instructions to the colored troops as to the course they should pursue toward Confederate soldiers that might fall into their hands; but seeing no disavowal on the part of the Confederate Government, but on the contrary laudations from the entire Southern press of the perpetrators of the massacre, I may safely presume that indiscriminate slaughter is to be the fate of colored troops that fall into your hands; but I am not willing to leave a matter of such grave import and involving consequences so fearful to interference, and I have therefor thought it proper to address you this, believing that you will be able to indicate the policy that the Confederate Government intends to pursue hereafter on this question. If it is intended to raise the black flag against that unfortunate race, they will cheerfully accept the issue. Up to this time no troops have fought more gallantly and none have conducted themselves with greater propriety. They have fully vindicated their right (so long denied) to be treated as men. I hope I have been misinformed in regard to the treatment they have received at the battle of Brice's Cross-Roads, and that the accounts received result rather from the excited imaginations of the fugitives than from actual fact. For the government of the colored troops under my command I would thank you to inform me, with as little delay as possible, if it is your intention or the intention of the Confederate Government to murder colored soldiers that may fall into your hands, or treat them as prisoners of war and subject to be exchanged as other prisoners.

I am, general, respectfully, your obedient servant,

C.C. WASHBURN,

Major-General, Commanding.

HEADQUARTERS DISTRICT OF WEST TENNESSEE,

Memphis, Tenn., June 19, 1864.

Maj. Gen. N.B. Forrest,

Commanding Confederate Forces:

GENERAL: Your communication of the 14th instant is received. The letter to Brigadier-General Buford will be forwarded to him.

In regard to that part of your letter which relates to colored troops, I beg to say that I have already sent a communication on the same subject to the officer in command of the Confederate Forces at Tupelo.

Having understood that Maj. Gen. S.D. Lee was in command there, I directed my letter to him. A copy of it I inclose.

You say in your letter that it has been reported to you "that all negro troops stationed at Memphis took an oath on their knees, in presence of Major-General Hurlbut and other officers of our army, to avenge Fort Pillow, and that they would show your troops no quarter." I believe that this is true that the colored troops did take such an oath, but not in the presence of General Hurlbut. From what I can learn, this act of theirs was not influenced by any white officer, but was the result of their own sense of what was due to themselves and their fellows, who had been mercilessly slaughtered. I have no doubt that they went into the field as you allege, in full beleif that they would be murdered in case they fell into your hands.

The affair of Fort Pillow fully justified that belief. I am not aware as to what they proclaimed on their late march, and it may be as you say, that they declared that no quarter would be given to any of your men that might fall into their hands. Your declaration that you have conducted the war on all occasions on civilized principals cannot be accepted, but I receive with satisfaction the intimation in your letter that the recent slaughter of colored troops at the battle of Tishomingo Creek resulted rather from the desperation with which they fought than a predetermined intention to give them no quarter. You must have learned by this time that the attempt to intimidate the colored troops by indiscriminate slaughter has signally failed, and that instead of a feeling of terror you have aroused a spirit of courage and despiration that will not down at your bidding.

I am left in no doubt by your letter as to the course you and the Confederate Government intend to pursue hereafter in regard to colored troops, and I beg you to advise me with as little delay as possible as to your intention. If you intend to treat such of them as fall into your hands as prisoners of war, please so state. If you do not so intend, but contemplate either their slaughter or their return to slavery, please state that, so that we may have no misunderstaning hereafter. If the former is your intention, I shall receive the announcement with pleasure, and shall explain the fact to the colored troops at once, and desire that they recall the oath that they have taken. If the latter is the case, then let the oath stand, and upon those who have aroused this spirit by their atrocities, and upon the Government and the people who sanction it, be the consequences.

In regard to your inquiry relating to prisoners of your command in our hands, I state that they have always receive the treatment which a great and human Government extend to its prisoners. What course will be pursued hereafter toward them them must of course depend on circumstances that may arise. If your command hereafter do nothing which should properly exclude them from being treated as prisoners of war, they will so be treated. I thank you for your offer to exchange wounded officers and men in your hands. If you will send them in I will exchange, man for man, so far as I have the ability to do so.

Before closing this letter I wish to call your attention to one case of unparalled outrage and murder that has been brought to my notice, and in regard to which the evidence is overwhelming. Among the prisoners captured at Fort Pillow was Major Bradford, who had charge of the defenses of the fort, after the fall of Major Booth. After being taken prisoner he was started with other prisoners in charge of Colonel Duckworth for Jackson [Tennessee]. At Brownsville they rested overnight. The following morning two companies were detailed by Colonel Duckworth to proceed to Jackson with the prisoners. After they had started and proceeded a very short distance, 5 soldiers were recalled by Colonel Duckworth and were conferred with by him. They then rejoined the column, and after proceeding about 5 miles from Brownsville the column was halted and Major Bradford taken about 50 yards from the roadside and deliberately shot by the 5 men who had been recalled by Colonel Duckworth, and his body left unburied upon the ground where he fell. He now lies buried near the spot, and if you desire, you can easily satisfy yourself of the truth of what I assert. I beg leave to say to you that this transaction hardly justifies your remark that your operations have been conducted on civilized principals, and until you take some steps to bring perpetrators of this outrage to justice the world will not fail to beleive that it had your sanction.

I am, general, respectfully, your obedient servant,

C.C. WASHBURN,

Major-General, Commanding.

HEADQUARTERS FORREST'S CAVALRY,
Tupelo, June 20, 1864.
Maj. Gen. C.C. Washburn,
Commanding U.S. Forces, Memphis:

GENERAL: I have the honor to acknowledge the receipt (per flag of truce) of your letter of the 17th instant, addressed to Maj. Gen. S.D. Lee, our officer commanding Confederate forces near Tupelo. I have forwarded it to General Lee with a copy of this letter.

I regard your letter as discourteous to the commanding officer of this department, and grossly insulting to myself. You seek by implied threats to intimidate him, and assume the privilege of denouncing me as a murderer and as guilty of the wholesale slaughter of the garrison at Fort Pillow, and found your assertions upon the ex parte testimony of your friends, the enemies of myself and country.

I shall not enter into discussion, therefor, of any of the questions involved nor undertake and refutation of the charges made by you against myself; nevertheless, as a matter of personal privilege alone, I unhesitatingly say that they are unfounded and unwarranted by the facts. But whether these charges are true or false, with the question you ask as to whether negro troops when captured will be recognized and treated as prisoners of war, subject to exchange, are matters which the Government of the United States and Confederate States are to decide and adjust, not their subordinate officers.

I regard the captured negroes as I do other captured property and not as captured soldiers, but as how regarded by my Government and the disposition which has been and will hereafter be made of them, I respectfully refer you through the proper channel to the authorities at Richmond. It is not the policy nor the interest of the South to destroy the negro-on the contrary, to preserve and protect him-and all who have surrendered to us have received kind and humane treatment.

Since the war began I have captured many thousand Federal prisoners, and they including the survivors of the Fort Pillow massacre (black and white), are living witnesses of the fact that with my knowledge or consent, or by order, not one of them has ever been insulted or in any way maltreated.

You speak of your forbearance in not giving your negro troops instructions and orders as to the course they should pursue in regard to Confederate soldiers that might fall into their (your) hands, which clearly conveys to my mind two very distinctive impressions. The first is that in not giving them instructions and orders you have left the matter intirely to the discretion of the negroes as to how they should dispose of prisoners; second, and implied threat to give such orderes as will lead to "consequences to fearful for contemplation." In confirmation of the correctness of the first impression (which your language now fully develops), I refer you most respectfully to my letter from battle-field of Tishomingo Creek and forwarded you by flag of truce on the 14th instant. As to the second impression, you seem disposed to take into your own hands the settlements which belong to, and can only be settled by, your Government, but if you are prepared to take upon yourself the responsibility of inaugurating a system of warfare contrary to civilized usages, the onus as well as the consequences will be chargeable to yourself.

Deprecating, as I should do, such state of affairs, determined as I am not to be instrumental in bringing it about, feeling and knowing as I do that I have the approval of my Governemnt, my people, and my own conscience, as to the past, and with the firm belief that I will be sustained by them in my future policy, it is left with you to determine what that policy shall be-whether in accordance with the laws of civilized nations or in violation of them.

I am, general, yours, very respectfully,

N.B. FORREST,
Major-General.

HEADQUARTERS FORREST'S CAVALRY,

In the Field, June 23, 1864.

Maj. Gen. C.C. WASHBURN,

Commanding U.S. Forces, Memphis, Tenn.:

GENERAL: Your communication of the 19th instant is received, in which you say "you are left in doubt as to the course the Confederate Government intends to pursue hereafter in regard to colored troops."

Allow me to say that this is a subject upon which I did not and do not propose to enlighten you. It is a matter to be settled by our Governments through their proper officers, and I respectfully refer you to them for a solution of your doubts. You ask me to state whether "I contemplate either their slaughter or their return to slavery." I answer that I slaughter no man except in open warfare..., and that my prisoners, both white and black, are turned over to my Government to be dealt with as it may direct. My Government is in possession of all the facts as regards my offical conduct and the operations of my command since I entered the service, and if you desire a proper discussion and decision, I refer you again to the President of the Confederate States.

I would not have you understand, however, that in a matter of so much importance I am disposed to place at your command and disposal any facts desired, when applied for in a manner becoming an officer holding your rank and position., for it is certainly desirable to every one occupying a public position to be placed right before the world, and there has been no time since the capture of Fort Pillow that I would not have furnished all the facts connected with its capture had they been applied for properly; but now the matter rests with the two Governments. I have, however, for your information, inclosed you copies of the official correspondence between the commanding officers at Fort Pillow and myself; also copies of a statement of Captain Young, the senior officer of that garrison (Captain Young's letter mentioned here, follows this letter), together with (sufficient) extracts from a report of the affair by my aide-de-camp, Capt. Charles W. Anderson, which I approve and indorse as correct.

As to the death of Major Bradford, I knew nothing of it until eight or ten days after it is said to have occured. On the 13th (the day after the capture of Fort Pillow) I went to Jackson, and the report that I had of affair was this: Major Bradford was with other officers sent to the headquarters of Colonel McCulloch, and all the prisoners were in charge of one of McCulloch's regiments. Bradford requested the privilege of attending the burial of his brother, which was granted, he giving his parole to return; instead of returning he changed his clothing and started for Memphis. Some of my men were hunting deserters, and came on Bradford just as he had landed on the south bank of the Hatchie, and arrested him. When arrested he claimed to be a Confederate soldier belonging to Bragg's army; that he had been home on furlough, and was then on his way to join his command. As he could show no papers he was believed to be a deserter and was taken to Covington, and not until he was recognized and spoken to by citizens did the gaurds know that he was Bradford. He was sent by Colonel Duckworth, or taken by him, to Brownsville. All of Chalmers command went south from Brownsville via LaGrange, and as all the other prisoners had been gone some time, and there was no chance to catch up and place Bradford with them, He was ordered by Colonel Duckworth or General Chalmers to be sent to me at Jackson. I knew nothing of the matter until eight or ten days afterward. I heard that his body was found near Brownsville. I understand that he tried to escape, and was shot. If he was improperly killed nothing would afford me more pleasure than to punish the perpetrators to the full extent of the law, and to show you how I regard such transactions I can refer you to demand upon Major-General Hurlbut (no doubt upon file in your office) for the delivery to Confederate authorities of one Col. Fielding Hurst and others of his regiment, who deliberately took out and killed 7 Confederate soldiers, one of whom they left to die after cutting off his tongue, punching out his eyes, splitting his mouth on each side to his ears, and cutting off his privates.

I have mentioned and given you these facts in order that you may have no further excuse or apology for referring to these matters in connection with myself,and to evince to you my determination to do all in my power to avoid the responsibility of causing the adoption of the policy which you seem determined to press.

In your letter you acknowledge the fact the the negro troops did take an oath on bended knee to show no quarter to my men; and you say further, "you have no doubt they went to the battlefield expecting to be slaughtered," and admit also the probability of their having proclaimed on their line of march that no quarter would be shown us. Such being the case, why do you ask for the disavowal on the part of the commanding general of this department or the Government in regard to the loss of life at Tishomingo Creek?

That your troops expected to be slaughtered, appears to me, after the oath they took, to be very reasonable and natural expectation. Yet you, who sent them out, knowing and now admitting that they had sworn to such a policy, are complainging of atrocities, and demanding ackowledgments and disavowals on the part of the very men you sent forth to slay whenever in your power. I will in all candor and truth say to you that I had only heard these things, but did not believe them to be true; at any rate, to the extent of your admission; indeed, I did not attach to them the importance they deserved, nor did I know of the threatened vengeance, as proclaimed along their lines of march, until the contest was over. Had I and my men known it as you admit it, the battle of Tishomingo Creek would have been noted as the bloddiest battle of the war. That you sanctioned this policy is plain, for you say now "that if the negro is treated as a prsoner of war you will receive with pleasure the announcement, and will explain the fact to your colored troops at once, and desire (not order) that they recall the oath; but if they are either to be slaughtered or returned to slavery, let the oath stand.

Your rank forbids a doubt as to the fact that you and every officer and man of your department is identified with this policy and responsible for it, and I shall not permit you, notwithstanding, by your studied language in both your communications, you seek to limit the operations of your un-holy scheme and visit its terrible consequences alone upon that ignorant, deluded, but unfortuntate people, the negro, whose destruction you are planning in order to accomplish ours. The negroes have our sympathy, and so far as consistent with safety will spare them at the expense of those who are alone responsible for the inauguration of a worse than savage warfare.

Now, in conclusion, I demand a plain, unqualified answer to two questions, and then I have done with further correspondence with you on this subject. This matter must be settled. In battle and on the battle-field, do you intend to slaughter my men who fall into your hands? If you do not intend to do so, will they be treated as prisoners of war? I have over 2,000 of Sturgis' command prisoners, and will hold every officer and private as hostage until I receive your declarations and am satisfied that you carry out in good faith the answers you make, and until I am assured that no Confederate soldier has been foully dealt with from the day of the battle at Tishomingo Creek to this time. It is not not yet to late for you to retrace your steps and arrest the storm.

Relying as I do upon that Divine Power which in wisdom disposes of all things; relying also upon the support and approval of my Government and countrymen, and the unflinching bravery and endurance of my troops, and with consciousness that I have done nothing to produce, but all in my power consistent with honor and the personal safety of myself and command to prevent it, I leave with you the responsibility of bringing about, to use your own language, "a state of afairs too fearful for contemplation."

I am, general, very respectfully, yours &c.,

N.B. FORREST,

Major-General.

CAHABA, ALA.,

May 19, 1864.

Major-General Forrest,

C.S. Army:

GENERAL: Your request, made through Judge P.T. Scruggs, that I should make a statement as to the treatment of Federal dead and wounded at Fort Pillow, has been made known to me. Details from Federal Prisoners were made to collect the dead and wounded. The dead were buried by their surviving comrades. I saw no ill-treatment of the wounded on the evening of the battle, or the next mourning. My friend, Lieutenant Leaming, adjutant Thirteenth Tennessee Cavalry, was left under the sutler's store near the Fort; also a lieutenant of the Sixth U.S. Artillary; both were alive the next morning and sent on board U.S. transport, among many other wounded. Among the wounded were some colored troops. I do not know how many.

I have examined a report said to be made by Captain Anderson, aide-de-camp to Major-General Forrest, appendix top General Forrest's report, in regard to making disposition of Federal wounded left on the field at Fort Pillow, and think it is correct. I accompanied Captain Anderson on the day succeeding the battle to Fort Pillow, for the purpose mentioned above.

Very respectfully, your obedient servant,

JOHN T. YOUNG,

Captain, Twenty-fourth Missouri Volunteers.

MEMPHIS, TENN.,

September 13, 1864.

Maj. Gen. C.C. WASHBURN,

Commanding District West Tennessee:

GENERAL: I have the honor to address you in regard to certain papers forwarded you by Major-General Forrest (regaurding the preceeding letter and statement made by Captain Young while in Cahaba prison), of the so-called Confederate Army, signed by me under protest while a prisoner of war at Cahaba, Ala.:

I would first call your attention to the manner by which those papers were procured about 27th April last. All Federal prisoners (except colored soliers) were sent to Andersonville and Macon, Ga., myself among the number. About ten days after my arrival at Macon prison, a Confederate captain, with 2 men as gaurd, came to that prison with an order to return me to Cahaba. I appealed to the officer in command to know why I was being taken from the other officers, but received no explanation. Many of my friends among the Federal officers who had been prisoners longer than myself felt uneasy at the proceeding, and advised me to make my escape going back, as it was likely a subject of retailiation. Consequently I felt considerable uneasiness of mind.

On returning to Cahaba, being quite unwell, I was placed in hospital under gaurd, with still no explanation from the military authorities. On the day following I was informed by a sick Federal officer, also in hospital, that he had learned that I had been in the volunteer service since 1st of May, 1861, I still felt uneasy, having fresh in my mind Fort Pillow, and the summary manner the Confederate officers have of disposing of men on some occasions.

With the above impressions on my mind, about three days after my return to Cahaba I was sent for by the provost-marshall, and certain papers handed to me, made out by General Forrest, for my signature. Looking over these papers I found that signing them would be an indorsement of General Forrest's official report of the Fort Pillow affair. I, of course, returned the papers, positivley refusing to have anything to do with them. I was sent for again the same day with request to sign other papers of the same tendancy, but modified. I again refused to sign the papers but sent General Forrest a statement, that although I considered some of the versions of the Fort Pillow affair which I had read in copies of Federal papers exaggerated, I also thought that his own offical report was equally so in some particulars. Here the matter rested about one week, when I was sent for by Col. H.C. Davis, commander of post at Cahaba, who informed me that General Forrest had sent Judge P.T. Scruggs to see me and have a talk with me about the Fort Pillow fight. I found the judge very affable and rather disposed to flatter me. He said that General Forrest thought that I was a gentleman and a soldier, and that the General had sent him (the judge) down to see me and talk to me about the Fort Pillow fight. He then went on to tell over a great many things that were testified to before the military commission which was I was perfectly ignorant of never having seen the testimony. He then produced papers which General Forrest wished me to sign. Upon examination I found them about the same as those previously shown me, and refused to sign them; but the judge was very importunate and finally prevailed on me to sign the papers you have in your possession, pledging himself that if I wished it they should only be seen by General Forrest himself; that they were not intended to be used by him as testimony, but merely for his own satisfaction.

I hope, General, that these papers signed by me, or rather extorted from me while under duress, will not be used by my Government to my disparabement, for my only wish now is, after over three years service, to recruit my health, which has suffered badly by imprisonment, and go in for the war.

I have the honor, general, to be your obedient servant,

JOHN T. YOUNG,

Captain Company A. Twenty-fourth Missouri Infantry.

HEADQUARTERS DISTRICT OF WEST TENNESSEE,
Memphis, Tenn., July 2, 1864.
Maj. Gen. N.B. FORREST,
Commanding Confederate Forces, near Tupelo:

GENERAL: Your communications of the 20th and 23rd utlimo are received. Of the tone and temper of both I do not complain. The desperate fortunes of a bad cause excuse much irritation of temper, and I pass it by. Indeed, I received it as a favorable augury and as evidence that you are not indifferent to the opinons of the civilized world.

In regard to the Fort Pillow affair, it is useless to prolong the discussion. I shall forward your report, which you did me the favor to inclose, to my Government, and you will receive the full benefit of it. The record is now made up, and a candid world will judge of it. I beg leave to send you, herewith, a copy of the report of the investigating committee from the U.S. Congress on the affair.

In regard to the treatment of Major Bradford, I refer you to the testimony contained in that report, from which you will see that he was not attempting to escape when shot. It will be easy to bring the perpetrators of the outrage to justice if you so desire. I will add to what I have heretofore said, that I have it from responsible and truthful citizens of Brownsville, that when Major Bradford was started under escort for your headquarters at Jackson, General Chalmers remarked that he "would never reach there." You call attention apparently as an offset to this affair of Major Bradford to outrages said to have been commited by Col. Fielding Hurst and others of his regiment (Sixth Tennessee Cavalry). The outrages, if committed as stated by you, are disgraceful and abhorrent to very brave and sensitive mind. On receiving your letter, I sent at once for Colonel Hurst, and read him the extract pertaining to him. He indignantly denies the charge against him, and until you furnish me the names of the parties murdered, and the time when, and the place where, the offense was commited, with names of witnesses, it is impossible for me to act. When you do that, you may rest assured that I shall use every effort in my power to have the parties accused tried, and, if found guilty, properly punished.

In regard to the treatment of colored soldiers, it is evidently useless to discuss the question further. Your attempt to shift from yourself upon me the responsibility of the inauguration of a "worse than savage warfare," is too strained and far-fetched to require any response. The full and cumulative evidence contained in the Congressional report I herewith forward, points to you as the person responsible for the barbarisms already committed.

It was your soldiers who at Fort Pillow raised the black flag, and while shooting, bayoneting, and otherwise maltreating the Federal prisoners in their hands, shouted to each other in the hearing of their victims that it was done by "Forrest's orders." Thus far, I cannot learn that you have made any disavowal of these barbarities. Your letters to me inform me confidently that you have always treated our prisoners according to the rules of civilized warfare, but your disavowal of the Fort Pillow barbarities, if you intend to make any, should be full, clear, explicit, and published to the world. The United States Government is, as it always has been, lenient and forbearing, and it is not yet too late for you to secure yourself and soldiers a continuance of the treatment due to honorable warriors, by public disclaimer of barbarities already commited, and a vigorous effort to punish the wretches who commited them. But I say to you now, clearly and unequivocally, that such measure of treatment as you mete out to Federal soldiers will be measured to you again. If you give no quarter, you must expect none; if you observe the rules of civilized warfare, and treat our prisoners in accordance with the laws of war, your prisoners will be treated, as they ever have been, with kindness. If you depart from these principals, you may expect such retaliation as the laws of war justify. That you may know what the laws of war are, as understood by my Government, I beg leave to inclose a copy of General Orders, no. 100, from the War Department, Adjutant-General's Office, Washington, April 24, 1863.

I have the honor to be, sir, very respectfully, yours,

C.C. WASHBURN,
Major-General.

HEADQUARTERS DISTRICT OF WEST TENNESSEE,
Memphis, Tenn., July 3, 1864.
Lieut. Gen. S.D. Lee, C.S. Army,
Comdg. Dept. Ala., Miss., and E. La., Meridian, Miss.:

GENERAL: Your letter of the 28th ultimo, in reply to mine of thge 17th ultimo, is received.

The discourtesy which you profess to discover in my letter I utterly disclaim. Having already discussed at length in a correspondence with Major-General Forrest the Fort Pillow massacre, as well as the policy to be pursued in regard to colored troops, I do not regard it necessary to say more on those subjects. As you state that you fully approve of the letter sent by General Forrest to me, in answer to mine of the 17th ultimo, I am forced to presume that you fully approve of his action at Fort Pillow. Your arguments in support of that action confirm such presumption. You state that the version given by me and my Government is not true, and not sustained by the facts to the extent I indicate. You furnished a statement of a certain Captain Young, who was captured at Fort Pillow, and is now a prisoner in your hands.

How far a statement of person under duress and in the position of Captain Young should go to disaprove the sworn testimony of the hundred eye-witnesses who had ample opportunity of seeing and knowing I am willing that others shall judge. In relying as you do upon the certificate of Captain Young, you confess that all better resources are at an end. You are welcome to all the relief that that certificate is calculated to give you. Does he say that our soldiers were not inhumanly treated? No. Does he say that he was in a posistion to see and know what took place, it is easy for him to say so.

Yesterday I sent to Major-General Forrest a copy of the report of the Congressional Investigating Committee, and I hope it may fall into your hands. You will find there the record of inhuman atrocities, to find parallel for which you will search the history in vain. Men (white men and black men) were crucified and burned; others were hunted by bloodhounds, while others in their anguish were made the sport of men more cruel than the dogs by which they were hunted. I have also sent to my Government copies of General forrest's reports, together with the certificate of Captain Young. The record in the case is plainly made up, and I leave it. You justify and approve it, and appeal to history for precedents,

As I have said, history furnishes no parrallels. True, there are instances where after a long and protracted resistance resulting in heavy loss to the assailing party, the garrison has been put to the sword; but I know of no such instance that did not bring dishonor upon the commanders that ordered or suffered it. There is no Englishman that would not gladly forget Badajos, nor a Frenchman that exults when Jaffa or the caves of Dahla and Shelas are spoken of. The massacre of Glencoe, which the world has read with horror for nearly two hundred years, pales into insignificance before the truthful recital of Fort Pillow. The desperate defense of the Alamo was the excuse for the slaughter of its brave survivors after its surrender; yet that act was received with just execration, and we are told by the historian that it led, more than anything alse, to the independence of Texas. At the battle of San Jacinto, the Texans rushed into action with the warcry, "Remember the Alamo!" and carried all before them. You will seek in vain for consolation in history, pursue the inquiry as far as you may. Your desire to shift the reponsibility of the Fort Pillow massacre, or to find excuses for it, is not strange. But the responsibility still remains where it belongs, and there it will remain.

In my last letter to General Forrest I stated that the treatment which Federal soldiers received would be their guide hereafter, and that if you give no quarter you need expect none. If you observe the rules of civilized warfare I shall rejoice at it, as no one can regret more than myself a resort to such measures as the laws of war justify toward an enemy that gives no quarter.

Your remark that our colored troops "will not be regaurded as prisoners of war, but will be retained and humanely treated," indicating that you consider them as of more worth and importance than your own soldiers who are now in our hands, is certainly very complimentary to our colored troops, though but a tardy ackowledgement of their bravery and devotion as soldiers; but such fair words can neither do justice to the colored soldiers who were butchered at Fort Pillow after they had surrendered to their victors, nor relieve yourself, General forrest, and the troops serving under you from the fearful responsibility now resting upon you for those wanton and unparalleled barbarities. I concur in your remark that if the black flag is once raised there can be no distinction so far as our soldiers are concerned. No distinction in this regard as to color is known to laws of war, and you may rest assured that the outrages we complain of are felt by our white soldiers, no less than by our black ones, as insults to their common banner, the flag of the United States.

I will close by reference to your statement that many of our colored soldiers "are yet wandering over the country attempting to return to their masters." If this remark is intended as a joke, it is ackowledged as a good one, but if stated as a fact, permit me to correct your misapprehensions by informing you that most of them have rejoined their respective commands, their search for their late "masters" having proved bootless; and I think I do not exaggerate in assuring you that there is not a colored soldier here who does not prefer the fate of his comrades at Fort Pillow to being returned to his "master."

I remain, general, yours, very respectfully,

C.C. WASHBURN,

Major-General.

The following letter from Lieutenant-General S.D. Lee, to General S. Cooper, Adjutant and Inspector General, C.S. Army, Richmond, Va.

HDQRS. DEPARTMENT ALA., MISS., AND EAST LA.,

Meridian, Miss., June 30 , 1864.

GENERAL: I have the honor to transmit copies of correspondence between General Washburn, U.S. Army, General Forrest, and myself, which I consisder very important and should be laid before the Department. It will be my endeavor to avoid, as far as is consistent with my idea of the dignity of my position, resorting to such an extremity as the black flag, and the onus shall be with the Federal commander. I would like that the onus be put where it properly belongs-before the public-should the extremity arise. The corrspondence is not complete yet, and the Department will be informed of the result at the earliest practible moment.

I am, general, yours, respectfully,

S.D. LEE.

Lieutenant-General.

The following letter from Confederate Secretary of War J.A. Seddon, to Confederate President Jefferson Davis.

JULY 28, 1864.

Respectfully submitted for the information of the President, who will probably be interested to see the grounds taken by our officers concerning the affair at Fort Pillow and the treatment of negro troops. The implied admissions of the Federal generals are infamous, and are properly exposed, especially in General Forrest's second letter, which though neither elegant nor strictly grammatical, is better, being very much to the point and in true spirit, The correspondence on the part of our officers meets my approval, and I trust, with yours.

J.A. SEDDON,
Secretary.

Confederate President Jefferson Davis read all correspondence between Forrest, Lee, and Washburn, up to that time, and returned all correspondence to Secretary of War Seddon, with the following letter.

JULY 30, 1864.
Returned to the Secretary of War.
The tone of the correspondence on the part of our officers is approved. Much misrepresentation of events connected with the capture of Fort Pillow has been thrown upon the world in the form of a report of a select committee of the two houses of the United States Congress. It is due to our Government that the truth should be sent out to correct the false impression extensively created. It might be well to have at least a part of these communications published, but they are susceptible of many useful additions to the testimony they contain. You will observe frequent and obvious errors, probably due to the copyists; the sense, however, is perceptible.

JEFFERSON DAVIS

As the war continued, there was little mention of the Fort Pillow affair after this line of correspondence.

CONFEDERATE OFFICERS SWORN STATEMENTS ON THE FORT PILLOW BATTLE

Due to the Northern version of the atrocities committed at Fort Pillow and the final victory for the North instead of the South in the Civil War, the Battle at Fort Pillow would forever be cause for argument on what acctually happened there. In the North, Nathan Bedford Forrest carried the label of a butcher and murderer of innocent Union Soldiers, in the South He was forever a hero and military genious due to his ability to out manuver and out smart the Union Army on pratically every occasion.

Forrest's unsuccessful attempt at a political and business carreer after the War was partially due to the North's refusal to forget the alledged atrocities commited at Fort Pillow, exagerated or not.

John Allen Wyeth, an ex-Confederate soldier himself and the Author of the book "That Devil Forrest life of Nathan Bedford Forrest" made many personal contacts with Forrest's Officers and men thirty plus years after the war, and these without exception, made a positive denial under oath of the story of the massacre which the report of the subcommittee of Congress asserted had taken place. The statements from the following Officers was taken from Wyeth's book.

General James R. Chalmers, member of the United States Congress since the war, a lawyer of Memphis, Tennessee, was second in command to General Forrest in this engagement. He swears that the charge of a massacre is absolutely false; that those of the garrison who were sober enough to realize tha hopelessness of their situation after the fort was stormed, surrendered, and thus escaped being killed or wounded; that General Forrest rushed into the fort as quickly as he could ride from the position he occupied at the time of the assualt, and while the firing was going on beneath the bluff, and after the surrender of most of the whites and some sixty negroes had taken place, he gave orders to stop the firing, which was done immediatley. One Confederate within his observation, who disregarded this order, he personally arrested and placed under guard for the offense.

Some of the Federals, mostly negroes, who in fright or desperation broke through the Confederates in the effort to escape, were pursued and shot, as were those who attempted to escape by swimming down the river. Some of these were killed and some few succeded in getting away. He further testifies, "The Fedral flag was not lowered and no surrender of the garrison was ever made. As the Federals rushed down the bluff they carried their guns with them, and many of them turned and fired as they retreated, and continued to fire beneath the bluff, and these were the only men shot after the flag was hauled down."

Brigadier General Tyree H. Bell, now a prominent citizen of fresno, California, was in command of the right wing of the assaulting column and was among the first to reach the interior of the fort. He states, under oath: "The bugle sounded, and our command moved at once to the assault and scaled the walls of the fort, each man with his gun and navy-six loaded, the garrison firing continuously as they went over. Our troops never fired a gun until they landed inside the fort. The firing lasted not exceeding three minutes, and there was no more firing from either side. I went over the parapet with my men, and the first thing I noticed after the firing ceased was three or four vessels of whiskey with tin cups attached."

General Bell further testifies that he had these vessels overturned to prevent his troops from getting at the liquor, and that General Forrest galloped to the fort almost immediately after the Confederates had gained entrance and ordered the firing to cease. "The captured prisoners were then detailed to bury their dead. Between sunset and dark we moved out with our command and the prisoners, and camped about fifteen miles back in the country. The drunken condition of the garrison and the failure of Colonel (Major) Bradford to surrender, thus necessitating the assault, were the causes of the fatality. [In some recruiting papers in the author's possession, taken at Fort Pillow, this officer signs his name W.F. Bradford, Colonel.] The statements in relation to alledged 'cruelty and barbarism' practiced by Forrest's command are a tissue of lies from end to end."

Colonel Robert McCulloch, who commanded the left wing of the Confederates, now living at Clark's Fork, near Booneville, Missouri, and at this date Major General of the Missouri Division of United Confederate Veterans, swears that there was no massacre at Fort Pillow, and that nothing occured during or after the engagement which, with due regard for fairness and truth of history, could be construed into a massacre. "Not a gun was fired, nor a prisoner or non-combatant shot, to my knowledge or belief, after the surrender was made. I do solemnly swear that I was a member of the command of General N.B. Forrest, and was present at, and took part in, the capture of Fort Pillow, on April 12, 1864. That the testimony of certain witnesses made before the subcommitee of the United States Congress soon after the battle in 1864, stating that a massacre of the garrison took place after the fort was captured, is false. The presence of open whiskey barrels within the fort, together with the conduct of the troops after the Confederates had carried the works, showed plainly that a large portion of the garrison were under the influence of liquor at the time of the assault. The Federal flag flying over the fort was not lowered until after the garrison had fled for refuge under the bluff immediately behind the works, and no surrender was made by any officer of the garrison. As the Federal soldiers rushed for the bluff they carried their guns with them, and many of them turned and fired at us as they retreated, and some continued to fire from the crowd below the bank."

Colonel C.R. Barteau, one of Forrest's most gallant and trusted subordinates, at present (1899) practicing law in Memphis, Tennessee, commanded the Second Tennessee in Bell's brigade, and went over the works with his soldiers. It was from his troops that the detail of about two hundred men was made to take posistion below the bank near Cold Creek ravine. In his affidavit he states that a number of Federals, after others had surrenderd, continue to fight beneath the bluff until they were shot down. "They were in a frenzy of excitement or drunken delirium. Some even, who had thrown down their arms, took them up again and continued firing. Some of my own men had to take down the flag [Private John doak Carr, who died in 1897, at Hartsville, Tennessee.] The Federals did not do it, nor at any time make a surrender. During the truce they openly defied us from the breastworks to come and take the fort. All was done that could be done by General Forrest and his subordinates to save unnecessary loss of life and protect all who surrendered as soldiers in good faith. General Forrest deprecated the great slaughter that had taken place, and I heard him tell the prisoners it was the fault of their officers. The prisoners were placed in my charge, to be taken to Tupelo. Almost without exception they blamed their officers for the great loss of life. They told me that they had been led to believe that if they surrendered they would be killed by Forrest, and they were surprised and gratified at their humane treatment. On route south, to relieve their fatigue, I had my own men dismount at times and let prisoners ride."

Major Charles W. Anderson was at the time of the fight Captain and acting Adjutant General of the command. He now resides at florence, in Rutherford County Tennessee, and is President of the Confederate Veterans of that state. As he took such a prominent part in the encounter which occured beneath the bluff, his affidavit is given in full:

"I, Charles W. Anderson, of Florence, Rutherford County and State of Tennessee, do solemnly swear that I was at the time Captain of the Cavalry and acting Adjutant-General on the staff of General N.B. Forrest, and was the only member of the staff with him at the capture of Fort Pillow, April 12, 1864. Before the assault on the works I was temporarily placed in command of three companies of dismounted men from McCulloch's brigade, and ordered to take position on the face of the bluff just below the fort, and prevent the landing of steamers (then approaching) during truce.

"When Forrest's last and imperative demand for immediate surrender was refused, the general in person ordered me to "hold my position on the bluff, prevent any escape of the garrison by water, to pour rifle-balls into the open ports of the *New Era* when she went into action, and to *fight everything blue betwixt wind and water until yonder flag comes down.'*

When driven from the works, the garrison retreated towards the river, with guns in hand, and firing back, and as soon as in view we opened fire on them, and continued it rapidly until the Federal flag came down, when the firing was stopped at once, the detachment ordered back to their regiment, and in less than two minutes after the flag came down I joined the general inside the works.

"To the best of my knowledge and belief if did not exceed twenty minutes from the time our bugles sounded for the assault until the fort was in our possession and firing had ceased on every part of the ground.

"I further swear that six cases of rifle ammunition were found on the face of the bluff, in the immediate rear of the fort, with tops removed and ready for immediate distribution and use; also that about two hundred and seventy-five serviceable rifles and carbines were gathered up between the water's edge and the brow of the bluff, where they had been thrown down by the garrison when they found the gunboat New Era had deserted them and escape impossible. As my command did the most destructive as well as the very last firing done at Fort Pillow, the testimony of certain witnesses made before a sub-committee of the United States Congress, that a massacre of the garrison took place after capture, is false, and I further swear that to the best of my knowledge and belief tha heavy loss in killed and wounded during retreat was alone due to the incapacity of their commander, the drunken condition of the men, and the fatal agreement with and promise of Captain Marshall of the *New Era* to protect and succor them when driven from the works.

"Charles W. Anderson

"State of Tennessee,

County of Rutherford

"Personally appeared before me, W.H. Hindman, Notary Public of Rutherford County and State of Tennessee, Charles W. Anderson, of said County and State, who makes oath to the facts set forth in the above statement this February 23, 1898.

ANDERSONVILLE PRISON

The construction of Andersonville Prison began in early January of 1864 by James Winder, an amateur engineer named Hays and a nearby overseer, J.M. McNealy supervising the slave gangs.

First the woodchoppers began leveling pines, dragging the limbed trunks to a central location where teams of slaves armed with broadaxes and adzes scored and squared them into posts at least twenty feet long. When they cleared the ground where the prison was to be located and a sufficient amount of ground out away from the prison location, the work gangs traded their axes and bucksaws for shovels, opening a five-foot-deep trench around the perimeter of driven stakes marking the location of where the walls should be erected, pulling or hacking out only those stumps that sat in the path of their planned trapezoid. With the ditch completed Mr. Hays had the slaves turn his hewn beams upright, starting at the northern corners, while a separate crew followed along behind, filling and tamping.

On the west wall, above and below the stream which later became "stockade creek" Winder located a pair of gates, each of them surrounded on the outside with their on little stockade and another gate. That would allow one portal to always remain barred whenever prisoners or supplies entered. At intervals of ninety feet around the enclosure, carpenters perched six-by-four-foot pole platforms on the outside of the wall, about three feet beneath its upper edge. These "Pidgeon Roosts," as the prisoners came to call them, sported sloped shed roofs made of rough boards. Here the guards would stand, or lean their elbows on the log ends, counting the minutes until they could climb back down the ladders.

The prison was officially opened and had received its first lot of Union prisoners on February 24 1864.

Henry Wirz was commissioned to take command of Andersonville Prison by a Colonel Persons on March 29th 1864. Wirz and his wife Elizabeth Wolf, Ne'e Savells who

Captain Henry Wirz,
Prison Commandant

Brigadier General John H. Winder,
Andersonville Prison Post Commander

was from Cadiz Kentucky and had two daughters from a previous marriage had taken residence in the small town of Andersonville.

Wirz was an explosive and profane man, but the most credible testimony paints him as fair, with an occasional glint of kindness.

He was at the post early each day and there was a good deal to be done when he first assumed his duties, and the chores multiplied with each passing month; as the only officer directly connected with the prison, he worked every day of the week and often into the night. From the first he did not like the job, largely because he lacked sufficient authority to demand the materials he needed to meet his responsibilities.

One of Wirz first project was the construction of a "dead line." With free access to the walls around the stockade the prisoners would have little trouble undermining the logs, toppling them, and rushing the guard, or they could very easily tunnel under it and simply escape—especially in the stiffer clay north of the branch. Wirz's dead line might not solve all those problems altogether, but it would hamper such attempts severely. He began by ordering stakes driven into the ground parallel to the stockade and fifteen feet inside it. Pieces of scantling eventually connected the tops of those stakes, completing a fragile fence that defined the limits of the prisoners' range, and anyone who ventured across it was liable to be shot.

One of Wirz worst problems was sanitation within the stockade. With more than seven thousand (later to reach thirty thousand) men confined in sixteen acres, a fetid odor hung over the entire pen. Latrines, like the two near the hospital built inside the prison, might have contained the excrement, where it could be periodically limed and buried, but Wirz could not get the loan of so much as a shovel. The prisoners consequently used the only portion of the interior in which they could not build shelters, where the branch—now unofficially dubbed Stockade Creek—had been somewhat dammed by the upright logs used for the prison walls. This broad, swampy basin quickly evolved into the most obnoxious open sewer. At other places too distant from the creek for convenience, prisoners stricken suddenly by the call of nature scooped little pits with their bare hands, but those pits soon overflowed; those to lazy or ill to observe even such minimal sanitary concessions began to pollute the prison indiscriminately, some gouging little holes with their heels and fouling the interiors of their own shelters.

Colonel persons finally snagged some shovels in Augusta Georgia and returned with them to present to Wirz. Wirz distributed the shovels to two platoons of prisoners whom he assigned to clean up the ordure daily. They still had to dump the refuse in the extremity of the stream, but Wirz came up with an idea that might reduce that annoyance, too: he wanted to build two dams on the upper part of the creek, their elevation staggered like a pair of locks, both of which he planned to open each day to flush out the accumulated filth. The uppermost dam would provide a reservoir of clean drinking water, while the lower pool could be used for bathing. filled with dry clay, the banks of such a flume could also be spanned by a foot bridge, which would relieve the prisoners from having to wade through two feet of muck to collect water or visit across the creek.

Captain Winder still planned to build barracks, but lumber continued to elude him. He complained to the Macon Quartermaster that a whole trainload of materials destined for Andersonville had been sitting in central Georgia for nearly a fortnight, just waiting for cars to bring it down. Colonel persons again interfered on behalf of his post quartermaster, contracting a million board feet with a Macon sawyer, but that lumber only came in driblets. The portion that did arrive found its way to the cookhouse, where Yankee carpenters on parole hammered the building together. Captain Winder consid-

Map of
"Camp Sumter"
Andersonville
Prison site

A Map of Andersonville

ered this camp kitchen more important than barracks, and justly so, for while most of the prisoners yet owned some sort of shelter, many of them had no means of cooking the raw rations issued to them.

Shelter was never made available for the prisoners and the men made homemade shelters called "shebangs" out of whatever they could put together mainly consisting of sticks for braces and shelter halves or clothing used as the roofs when attached to the braces, these small shelters would sometimes house as many as four or five men who would have just enough room to keep their upper bodies in under the shelter and leave the lower bodies exposed to whatever conditions the Georgia climate might have at that time.

Food in the prison consisted of rations of cornmeal, raw bacon, and beans. The cornmeal proved to be deadly as the Georgia grinding mills were not equipped with bolting cloth, so the meal was delivered with the cobb ground up in it. The shredded cobb turned hard and sharp as the meal dried, taking a toll on the delicate walls of sick men's intestines, which in turn caused the death of thousands of men through dysentery and diarrhea. Some of the men tried to remove as much of the coarse meal as possible by making homemade sifters by poking holes into metal canteen halves, most had no access to such materials.

The prison passed its ten thousand man capacity on the first day of May, but the trains kept coming; in order to assure enough food for everyone, Captain Armstrong would have to cut the overall portions.

On April 19th John Whitten, a Iowa color-bearer, made his first complaint about short rations at Andersonville, a day in which he recorded watching seven hundred more prisoners march in the gate *(Thomas and the other Fort Pillow prisoners could possibly have been in this group, if not this group, a group within the next day or two)*.

On the last day of April a Massachusetts Captain, Ira Sampson, who had been sent here by mistake (He should have been put off at Macon Georgia, with the other officers) could find no suitable words to describe the sight that met him as he arrived inside the gate of Andersonville Prison. "Tis horrible," is all he scribbled in a pocket diary, jotting down his slightly inflated estimate of twelve to fifteen thousand men crowded into what looked like sixteen acres. He found a few square feet of open ground, soggy with recent rains, and at dark he lay down, trying to forget his predicament by staring at the bright fingernail of a waning moon.

By May prisoners were dying at a rate of nearly twenty a day. The bodies were carried out the south gate and more than a half of a mile north, where the post commander was turning Ben Dyke's land into a graveyard. The luxury of coffins was a thing of the past, and now they laid the bodies shoulder-to-shoulder in trenches, like a recumbent line of battle. The gravediggers could still not bear to throw dirt directly on the lifeless faces, though - not even Yankee faces. To compensate for a lack of lumber, the workman dug a seven-foot swath three feet deep, then left a six inch shoulder on either side while going down another foot. Placing the day's dead on the floor of this indented pit, they covered them with puncheons-slabs of rough-split pine-that rested on those shelves, forming a common (if somewhat leaky) casket.**

Thomas died on the 14th day of July, some details of what was happening inside the prison during his last days alive was taken from a diary of Sergeant James H. Dennison who provides a day by day description of his own experience there.

** *Andersonville The Last Depot - Marvel*

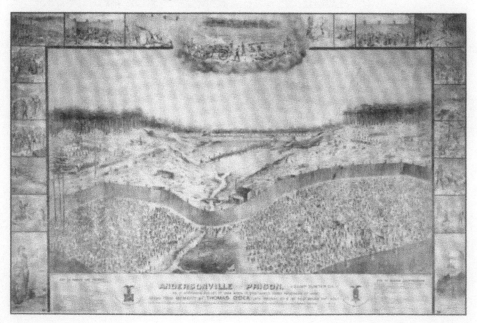

Burying the dead in mass graves without coffins.

Friday July 1st:

This is a fine morning the men still is dying off about half of the men moved up in the new addition there is plenty of wood the new addition at the north end has about 10 acres in extent, bringing the total area to about 26 1/2 acres. There were more than 26,000 prisoners in the camp at this time. By August, there were more than 32,000 men in the same space.

Saturday July 2nd:

This has been a warm day I feel well we have got a good place here it is good deàl better than whare we was first we get raw rations now we get more than we did.

Sunday July 3rd:

This is a warm day I feel well roal call for the first time thare was one man shot he went over the ded line some more prisoners came in 100.

Monday July 4th:

This is a nice cool morning it raines thay are taken our names again no selebration hear [i.e. of independence day] thay are giving us beef that stinks rain is verry hard.

Tuesday July 5th:

I feel well fine morning we are crowded hear thare is as meney dying hear yeat as thare was when we came hear, a bout 60 a day we are wating patiently for to get out of hear.

Wednesday July 6th:

This is a warm day we will get some vinegar I feel well and thank god for it thare was some more prisnors came in thare is very litel human nature hear among prisnors.

Thursday July 7th:

This is a warm morning I feel well thare is a good deal of quarling hear a mong the prisnors I feel bad to see it hear we get plenty meal.

we expect that sum of us will get out of hear to day I do have some pleasant dreams I think that I am to home with my wife but when I wake up I find myself still in prison in Georgey.

Friday July 8th:

Fine morning thare is a great many cars at the station last knight thare is a great many troops came in hear in the last few days.

Saturday July 9th:

This is a fine morning I feel well men dy as fast as 50 per day more prisnors it rained awful hard men has to suffer when it raines more prisnors 1250 [may be 250].

Sunday July 10th:

It is warm more prisnors from Grants six hundred taken at Petersburg I sent a letter home I fell well sleep cold at knight.

Monday July 11th:

Men dyes very fast hear now one hundred dyed the other day diarrhea is what they all dy from, then scurvy six men was hung for murder one broke the rope six men blonging to our armey was hung for murder hear in camp I saw them hung one of them broke the rope and fell to the ground [these were the leaders of the raiders, a gang of Union thugs who robbed and murdered other fellow prisoners].

Tuesday July 12th:

Warm morning more prisnors from Grant a bout 500 men still dyeing hear fast a bout 60 a day I feel well thank god for it.

Wednesday July 13th:

Two men shot this morning thay crost the ded line one of them died verry hot I feel well.

Thursday July 14th (this is the day Thomas died):

Warm this morning the Rebels is fraid we will try to get out of hear thare is prisnors hear now 28,440 thare is a bout 27 acres in this camp.

The rebels fell in line hear thay fired the canon thay went a round the camp and fired a few volleys I think thay are getting a fraid of us hear now I was to preaching this evening for the first time since I came hear.@@

Note: James H. Dennison did survive Andersonville and returned home after the war.

After Thomas witnessed the annihilation of his own unit at Fort Pillow, he could not have known that this was the beginning of the end, it would be impossible to know how he felt during his three months at Andersonville prison, As Thomas O' Day said, for a period of 12 months I resided in the "Prison Pens" of the South, as a "Guest" of the "Confederacy." There is not a man born that can accurately describe the scenes and sufferings of those who were imprisoned in those southern hells. One had to be there to witness and understand it!

@@ *Dennison's Andersonville Diary - Dennison*

No documented accounts were found from the 13th Tennessee Cavalry (Bradfords Battalion) while imprisoned at Andersonville, however through testimony from descendants, Thomas did manage to write at least two letters to his wife Maranda with descriptions of the deplorable conditions there, and how he and others were forced through starvation to eat anything, including rats should one venture into the stockade.~~~ Thomas died in the hospital of Andersonville Prison on July 14th 1864 of diarrhea c, he is buried at the Andersonville Cemetery in Section J, his grave stone number is 3328. Thomas's younger brother David Burton also died in the hospital at Andersonville prison on the 11th day of October 1864, he died of scorbutus (scurvy).

~~~ *Information provided by Clifton Ray-great grandson.*

13TH TENNESSEE CAVALRY U.S. THAT DIED IN ANDERSONVILLE PRISON

NAME	COMPANY	DATE DEATH	NUMBER	RANK	CAUSE OF DEATH
1. Peter Antoine	A	8/23/1864	6541	Privt	Dysentery C.
2. Thomas F. Burton	A	7/14/1864	3328	3rd Serg	Diarrhea C.
3. David M. Burton	A	10/11/1864		Corp	Scorbutus
4. James Clark	A	9/01/1864	7525	Privt	Anasarca
5. Ephraim churchwell	A	10/11/1864	10654	Privt	Scorbutus
6. James Childers	A	6/03/1864	1574	Privt	Rubeola
7. Randolph C. Gunter	A	9/01/1864	7454	1st D.Serg	Dysentary C.
8. Joseph Halford	A	9/07/1864	8094	Privt	Scorbutus
9. Garrett Haynes	A	8/21/1864	6393	Privt	Dysentary
10. John E. Lemmons	A	7/23/1864	3830	Privt	Diarrhea
11.John W. Long	A	8/02/1864	4575	Privt	Scorbutus
12.William T. Lovett	A	5/19/1864	1223	Privt	Rubeola
13.Valentia V. Matheny	A	9/26/1864	9783	5th Serg	Scorbutus
14.James W. Minger	A	7/20/1864	3642	Privt	Dysentary
15.Marcus Mitchum	A	6/25/1864	2475	Privt	Fever Typhus
16.James M. Moore	A	9/02/1864	7574	Privt	Diarrhea
17.Samuel Stafford	A	10/06/1864	10409	Privt	Anasarca
1. William C. Aspray	B	9/02/1864	7572	Privt	Diarrhea
2. Issac Baker	B	8/11/1864	5294	Privt	Dysentary
3. George W. Bowles	B	8/17/1864	6003	Privt	Anasarca
4. Dempsey Burris	B	7/20/1864	3636	Privt	Anasarca
5. Thomas H. Byrd	B	9/08/1864	8222	Privt	Anasarca
6. John H. Byron	B	7/14/1864	3330	Privt	DiarrheaC.
7. Andrew Crawford	B	6/21/1864	2289	Privt	Diarrhea
8. James Edson	B	10/16/1864	10985	Fifer	Scorbutus
9. James Ellington	B	10/30/1864	11639	Privt	Scorbutus
10.William Ethridge	B	8/16/1864	5904	Privt	Diarrhea
11.William Flowers	B	8/20/1864	6299	Serg	DiarrheaC.
12.Elbert Jones	B		7447	Serg	Dysentary
13.James Jones	B	9/12/1864	8503	Serg	Scorbutus
14.Andrew McKee	B	9/04/1864	764	Privt	Diarrhea
15.William Miffen	B	8/15/1864	5782	Privt	Diarrhea
16.Thomas L. Perry	B	7/01/1864	2748	Privt	Dysentary
17.Samuel Ray	B	6/18/1864	2132	Privt	Scorbutus
18.John A.H. Scoby	B	9/04/1864	7787	Privt	Dysentary
19.Robert M. White	B	9/02/1864	7618	Privt	DiarrheaC.
1. H. Bowels	C	7/25/1864	3934	Privt	Diarrhea
2. Alderson Cornish	C	8/04/1864	4691	Privt	Anasarca
3. Nathaniel G. Henderson	C	9/17/1864	9044	Privt	DiarrheaC.
4. John Jones	C	6/01/1864	1536	Privt	Diarrhea
5. Henry S. Morris	C	8/11/1864	5282	Privt	Diarrhea
7. Andrew Myers	C	8/18/1864	5008	Privt	Diarrhea
8. Thomas E. Needham	C	9/24/1864	9640	Blacksmith	DiarrheaC.
9. Joseph Norman	C	5/20/1864	1237	Corporal	Rubeola
10.James Profett	C	5/31/1864	2767	Privt	Diarrhea C.
11.William B. Pursley	C	7/02/1864	2767	Serg	Diarrhea
12.James T. Rice	C	5/29/1864	1450	Privt	Diarrhea C.
13.William Ryder	C	8/22/1864	6409	Corporal	Diarrhea

14.James A. Smith	C	9/18/1864	9192	Privt	Diarrhea
15.Jasper Southerland	C	9/20/1864	9381	Privt	Scorbutus
16.William P. Stafford	C	5/21/1864	254	Privt	Rubeola
17.William L. Tate	C	8/14/1864	5646	Privt	Diarrhea
18.John W Tidwell	C	8/05/1864	4825	Privt	Fever Remittant
1. Paton S. Alexander	D	9/11/1864	8493	Privt	Diarrhea
2. Benjamin Allison	D	6/22/1864	2313	Privt	Diarrhea C.
3. James H. Brown	D	1/31/1865	12565	Privt	Scorbutus
4. James W. Gibson	D	9/27/1864	9875	Privt	Scorbutus
5. Joseph C. Green	D	8/26/1864	6897	Privt	
6. Daniel S. Head	D	4/21/1864	660	Privt	Diarrhea
7. Charles Hogueley	D	6/23/1864	2375	Privt	Dysentery A.
8. William Johnson	D	2/26/1865	12702	Privt	Scorbutus
9. Bunyon J. Kirk	D	7/21/1864	3702	Privt	Diarrhea C.
10.Samuel Pankey	D	7/11/1864	3170	Bugler	Diarrhea
11.Thaddeus B. Paschall	D	8/03/1864	4592	Privt	Diarrhea
12.Jefferson Runnage	D	9/22/1864	9513	Privt	Dysentery
13.Levi Smith	D	8/13/1864	5462	Privt	Scorbutus
14.Edward Stewart	D	9/20/1864	9395	Bugler	Scorbutus
15.John Taylor	D	7/17/1864	3460	Privt	Scorbutus
16.Franklin Tidwell	D	2/22/1865	12694	Privt	Pleuritis
17.Jonathan Wilson	D	8/05/1864	4793	Privt	Scorbutus
1. J. Brown	E	6/05/1864	1635	Privt	Diarrhea
2. M.A. Baker	E	8/14/1864	5617	Privt	Dysentery C.
3. Henry C. Carter	E	7/05/1864	2940	Privt	Diarrhea C.
4. Ed Uriah Childers	E	9/01/1864	7523	Privt	Scorbutus
5. Thomas T. Cothram	E	9/05/1864	7851	Privt	Gangrene
6. Curtis Ellis	E	8/05/1864	4785	Privt	Scorbutus
7. James A. Haines	E	7/07/1864	3012	Privt	Diarrhea
8. J.J. Hall	E	8/06/1864	4855	Privt	Diarrhea C.
9. J.H. Hasborough	E	8/14/1864	5607	Privt	Scorbutus
10.John Hodges	E	9/26/1864	9788	Privt	Diarrhea C.
11.Wiley G. Poston	E	10/05/1864	10364	Serg	Scorbutus
12.J.F. Ralf	E	6/10/1864	1783	Privt	Diarrhea C.
13.Richard Richerdson	E	9/30/1864	10107	Privt	Scorbutus
14.S.H. Scarborough	E	7/08/1864	10454	Privt	Dysentery
15.John Shonnatt	E	10/07/1864	10454	Privt	Scorbutus
16.Joseph M. Smith	E	6/21/1864	2284	Privt	Diarrhea C.
17.Jessie W. Stewart	E	8/30/1864	7296	Privt	Dysentery
18.Andrew Sutton	E	8/14/1864	5625	Privt	Diarrhea
1. Moses J. Johnston	G	10/07/1864	10479	Privt	Scorbutus
2. John S. Walker	G	9/21/1864	9479	Privt	Diarrhea
1. H. Clay	H	10/03/1864	10268	Privt	Diarrhea
2. Thomas Woods	H	3/15/1865	12779	Privt	Scorbutus
1. Lewis H. Oliver	K	10/11/1864	10743	Privt	Diarrhea

Original photograph of the main road leading from the railroad depot in the city of Andersonville to the stockade. 50,000 Americans made this journey. For 12,000 prisoners and over a hundred guards, it was a one way trip.

Present day photo of road from depot to stockade.

119

Interior of Prison

Living along the Deadline 1864

Stockade Interior looking North along the stockade latrine.

View of stockade interior. Note man wearing suspenders at lower left.

Interior of stockade. The creek at the east side looking northwest.

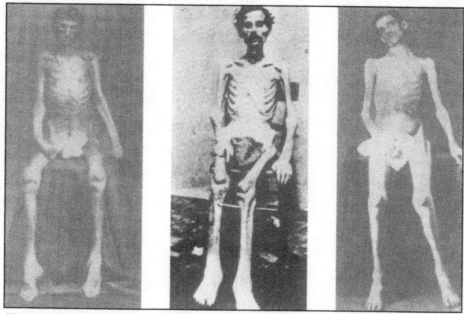

Victims of the conditions of southern prisons. Such extreme cases of malnutrition and scurvy existed in northern prisons as well.

Photo of Andersonville train tracks looking north.

Present day Andersonville Train Depot.

Photo of Andersonville railroad track and depot crossing.

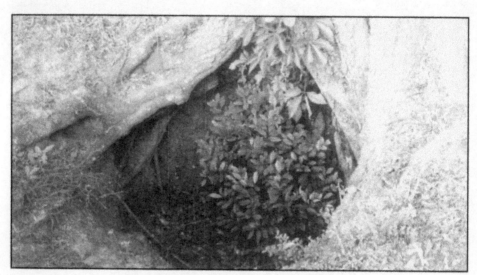

Photo of tunnel prisoners dug that caved in.

Photo of stockade creek and south end of prison interior toward hospital site.

Photo taken from inside Andersonville prison, stones are on original location of the south gate.

Reconstructed prison wall, pidgeon roost, deadline, and shabang.

Photo of stockade creek from outside Andersonville prison, this ditch served as a source for drinking, washing, and sanitation for up to 30,000 men during one time. Notice the white stakes in this picture, they mark the location of the deadline.

Photo of recreated north gate, shebang, and deadline. All recreated walls and deadline are on the exact spot of the originals.

Andersonville prison ceased to exist when the war ended in April and May 1865. Some former prisoners remained in Federal service, but most returned to the civilian occupations they had before the war. During July and August 1865, Clara Barton, a detachment of laborers and soldiers, and former prisoner named Dorence Atwater, came to Andersonville cemetary to identify and mark the graves of the Union dead. As a prisoner, Atwater was assigned to record the names of deceased Union soldiers for Confederate prison officials. Fearing loss of the death records at war's end, Atwater made his own copy of the dead interred at Andersonville. Thanks to Atwater's list and the Confederate death records captured at the end of the war, only 460 of the Andersonville graves had to be marked "unknown U.S. Soldier."

Photo of stockade creek and south gate location. The south gate was used to remove the dead each day, they were removed through this gate and put into a shanty called the dead house, here they awaited the burial detail who would load the bodies in a wagon and carry them to the cemetary.

The south gate is also the location in which a group of men called Raiders where hung. The Raiders consisted of six ring leaders and hundreds of other men, generally composed of "bounty jumpers" and other undesirables, many from large northern cities. Operating in large groups these men would rob and murdered their fellow soldiers trying to steal food, money, or clothing. In July 1864 a large group of prisoners called the regulators banded together to oppose the raiders, which involved numerous fights and incidents, and held them in the south gate area of the prison with the camp commandant's permission. The raiders were put on trial for their deeds. A jury of twenty four Union sergeants found the six ring leaders guilty and sentenced them to be hung. The other captured Raiders were allowed back into the stockade and forgiven, after being forced to run a punishing gauntlet of angry prisoners.

Dorence Atwater   *Clara Barton*

Captain Henry Wirz, the camps commandant, was arrested and charged with conspiring with high Confederate officials to "impair and injure the health and destroy lives...of Federal prisoners" and "murder, in violation of the laws of war." Such conspiracy never existed, but public anger and indignation throughout the north over the condition at Andersonville demanded appeasement. Tried and found guilty by a military tribunal, Wirz was hanged in Washington, D.C., on November 10, 1865. (Today a monument honoring Wirz, stands in the town of Andersonville.)

The Andersonville prison sight reverted to private ownership in 1875. In December 1890 it was purchased by the Georgia Department of the Grand Army of the Republic, a Union Veterans organization. Unable to finance improvements needed to protect the property, this group sold it for $1.00 to the woman's Relief Corps, the national auxillary of the G.A.R.

The woman's Relief Corps made many improvements to the area with the idea of creating a memorial park. Pecan trees where planted to produce nuts for sale to help maintain the site, and States began erecting commemorative monuments. The WRC built the Providence Spring House in 1901 to mark the sight where, on August 9, 1864, a spring burst forth during a heavy rainstorm—an occurence many prisoners attributed to Divine Providence. The fountain bowl in the spring house was purchased by funds raised by former Andersonville prisoners.

In 1910 the Woman's Relief Corps donated the prison site to the people of the United States. It was administered by the war department and its successor, the Department of the Army, through 1970, when it was made a national historic site. The National Park Service took over administration on July 1, 1971.

Photo of Captain Henry Wirz execution.
Execution was within view of the Capital building in Washington DC.

I am dying, comrades dying
Far away from friends and home
In this rebel den I'm lying
Suffering, staring, all alone.
Oh this lonesome dreary prison
Oh this cruel, rebel den
Where our mothers' sons are lying
Treated more like dogs than men.
No warm shelters are about us
No green fields, in which to range
Oh God grant that those who love us
May compel them to exchange.
If I could but see my mother
Though upon the ground I be
Mingled with earth starving
It would not be so hard to die.
If I could get a letter
Or some news would only come
Oh, I know I would get better
If I could but hear from home.
And the brave and suffering soldier
Bowed his manly head and wept
On the cold ground of his prison
Ere in death he calmly slept.
Am I dreaming, comrades dreaming
Surely someone called my name
And thought I was coming
And would take me home again.
Nearer, they are coming nearer
But somehow my sight is dim
And I thought someone was coming
And I think I hear them sing.
Nearer, they are coming nearer
I can see them plainly now
Oh, thank God, they're bringing water
For my fevered lips and brow.
Where's the flag flown, old flag comrades
With its brave red, white, and blue
I may tell those white robed beings
I served my country true.
Is it home, it seems more lovely
Than the home that once was mine
And the streets like starlight
Oh, so dazzling bright they shine.

Grave of Thomas Franklin Burton,
Andersonville, Georgia

Poem written by an unknown Andersonville prisoner

CALLOWAY COUNTY 1870 CENSUS & OTHER PERSONAL ACCOUNTS

After the war Maranda and her son John lived with her brother James, William, and Maranda's sister Mary. William lost his left arm during the battle at Fort Pillow. With war pension from Maranda and William, and James and William running the farm, they did live fairly well considering the time in which they lived. I am sure that William told Maranda the details of the battle at Fort Pillow.

Name	Age	Occupation	Sex	State born	Died
1.James K. Polk Allbritten	28	Farmer	M	KY	1/19/1885
2.William H. Allbritten	31 Born 4/23/1832	Farmer	M	KY	12/11/1887
3.Mary Allbritten	26	Keeping House	F	KY	1930
4.Maranda Burton	37 Born 6/12/1832	Keeping House	F	KY	12/15/1887
5.John T. Burton	6 Born 1/7/1864	At Home	M	KY	05/01/1940
6.Mary D. Steeley	75 At Home		F	NC	

CALLOWAY COUNTY 1880 CENSUS & OTHER PERSONAL ACCOUNTS

Name	Age	Occupation	Sex	State born	Died
1. James K.Polk Allbritten	39	Farmer	M	KY	1/19/1885
2. William H. Allbritten	42 Born 4/23/1838	Brother	M	KY	12/11/1887
3. Mary Allbritten	35	Sister Single	F	KY	1930
4. Maranda	48 Born 6/12/1832	Sister Widow	F	KY	12/15/1887
5. John T. Burton	16 Born 1/7/1864	Nephew	M	KY	05/01/1940

Name	Age	Occupation	Sex	State born	Died
1. M.F. Allbritten	29	Widow	F	KY	
2. J.R.	10	Son	M	KY	
3. Edward	9	Son	M	KY	
4. Sara R. Burton	69	Widow/Mother of M.F.	F	NC	

NOTE: Thomas's Mother Sara and Thomas's Sister M.F.

Name	Age	Occupation	Sex	State born	Died
1. Isaac Allbritten	49	Farmer	M	KY	7/5/1912
2. S.P.	46	Wife	F	TN	
3. T.E.	23	Son	M	KY	
4. J.S.	21	Son	M	KY	
5. N.B.	12	Daughter	F	KY	

NOTE: Maranda's Brother Isaac's Family

Name	Age	Occupation	Sex	State born	Died
1.William Allbritten	40	Farmer	M	KY	
2. N.A.	42	Wife	F	KY	
3. A.L.	18	Daughter	F	KY	
4. J.V.	15	Son	M	KY	
5. I.M.	5	Daughter	F	KY	

NOTE: Thomas's sister Elizabeth step son's Family

MARANDA BURTON

Maranda Burton accompanied by her brother William H. Allbritten (William lost his left arm, due to a bullet wound, received during the battle of Fort Pillow) and another man by the name of T. L. Oliver applied for pension in Paducah Kentucky on the 15th day of December 1868. She was issued a certificate for eight dollars per month commencing July 15th 1864 and two dollars per month commencing July 25th 1866 per child until that child reaches the age of sixteen which in this case will be January 6th 1880.

Maranda never re-married, two of her brothers and one sister lived with her and her son until her death on December 15th 1887, she was 55 years old.

Maranda's brother William died at age 49, four days prior to Maranda's death, probably from the same illness. Maranda is buried at the cemetery beside the Missionary Baptist church in New Providence Kentucky. (East side of the big cedar tree), Maranda is buried by her family in this order: left to right: Hoyt Vernon Burton & William Loyd Burton (Infant sons of John Thomas & E.R. Burton) - Missing stone? - Maranda Burton - John Polk Allbritten - William H. Allbritten (13th TN Cavalry) - Willie? (Dau. of J.R. and Mary McCuistion) - Sara Allbritten, wife of Isaac Allbritten - Issac Allbritten.

Maranda was described by her grand children as being a strong and well respected women, a women that all her descendants would have been proud of.

Maranda Burton's grave
Stone has the following inscription:
MARANDA
Wife of Thomas F. Burton
Born: June 12, 1832
Died: Dec. 15, 1887

JOHN THOMAS BURTON

Maranda raised her son John Thomas Burton, he was Thomas and Maranda's only child, John Thomas Burton died May 1st 1940 and is buried in Mount Pleasant Cemetery in Buchanon Tennessee.

JOHN THOMAS BURTON'S FAMILY

Name	Date Of Birth	Date of Death
John Thomas Burton	01/07/1864	05/01/1940
1st wife:Emma Rispy Wilson Burton	10/11/1867	02/17/1902
children:		
1.Hontas	10/01/1887	07/02/1943
2.Lula	03/24/1889	07/27/1976
3.Beatrice (Beatie)	01/28/1891	01/30/1913
4.William Loyd	10/25/1895	09/25/1896
5.Hoyt William	10/06/1896	02/19/1897
6.Ola Francis	04/06/1899	08/08/1983
7.Connie Clifton	04/02/1901	06/25/1977
2nd wife: Maggie Tucker Burton/married 1908	06/03/1880	06/10/1957
children		
1.John Quinton	11/01/1909	
2.James (Jim) Richard	05/21/1914	06/18/1981

The house that Thomas and Maranda lived in and John Thomas Burton was born in was made of logs and the kitchen had a dirt floor. John Thomas built a new house on the same location in the late 18.00's (pictured). this house was torn down in 1957, and John Thomas's son John Burton built a new house in its place (pictured). A large amount of old clothing and other miscellaneous belongings that belonged to Thomas and Maranda were discarded into the old cistern covered in the back yard.

Photo of John Thomas Burton, Beatrice, Hontas, Lula, and 1st wife Emma. (Emma holding baby Loyd) House was built by John on the exact location of Thomas and Maranda's residence. Photograph taken sometime early in the year of 1896.

Burton family: Back row left to right: Walls Taylor, Fred Burton, Lula Burton, Ola Burton Ray, Connie Burton. Middle row left to right: Hontus Burton Taylor(holding daughter Estelle), Mary Burton, Mary (Aunt Sis) McCuiston, John Thomas Burton, Maggie Tucker Burton. Front row left to right: Lelon Burton, John Burton, Preston Taylor, Lawton Burton, Jim Burton.

Above: John Thomas Burton.
Right: John Thomas Burton's grave located at Mount Pleasant Cemetary in Buchanon, Tennessee

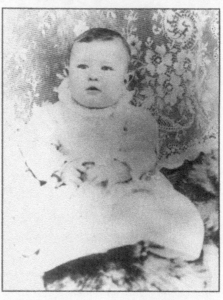

Beatrice (Beatie) Burton, John Thomas Burton's third daughter Beatrice died on January 30th, 1913 at the age of 22.

William Loyd Burton, John Thomas's 1st son by his first marriage to Emma Rispy Wilson Burton. William Loyd died on September 25th,1896 at age 11 months. Could not locate a photo of Hoyt William Burton who died at the age of 4 months.

Photograph of a 36 Cal. Whitney Navy Revolover, Thomas Burton and Carroll Sweeny both are holding a 36 Cal. Whitney Navy Revolver in the pictures they had made, most likley while they where at Fort Anderson in Paducah Kentucky. Eight to Ten thousand of these revolvers where issued by the Federal Ordinance Department to U.S. Cavalrymen during the Civil War.

John Quinton Burton, John Thomas's 1st son by his second marriage to Maggie Tucker Burton. Photo taken in 1997.

John Quinton Burton reidence. Location of Thomas and Maranda Burton's log home which was torn down by his son John Thomas Burton, John Thomas built a frame house on this location which was torn down by his son John Quinton Burton who resides at the same location today.

Photo of Lula Mae Burton and Fred Burton's children from left to right: Lelon Burton, Oleta Burton Swift, Eula Burton Hicks, and Lawton Burton, photograph taken in 1981.

Photo of Keith Black and John Suttles, John Suttles is the great great grandson of Carrol Sweeny who was a private in the Thirteenth Tennessee Cavalry Company A., U.S. Carrol Sweeny and Thomas Burton fought along side each other at the Fort Pillow Battle. Carrol Sweeny was also captured at Fort Pillow and taken to Andersonville Prison. Mr. Sweeny survived Andersonville and returned home after the war. John Suttles says that all he knows of Mr. Sweeny is that Mr. Sweeny was known for his fondness for gambling and that after the war he divorced his wife and left, never to be heard from again.

Photo looking East at the Allbritten Farm. State Line Road in the Middle, Kentucky on the left and Tennessee on the right.

137

MUSEUMS HOUSING INFORMATION ON THOMAS F. BURTON

KENTUCKY:
Columbus Belmont State Park was donated the following items:
1.Picture of Thomas F. Burton
2.All Military and Pension papers

TENNESSEE:
Fort Pillow State Park was donated the following items:
1.Picture of Thomas F. Burton (Presently on display in the Museum)
2.All Military and Pension papers

GEORGIA:
Andersonville State Park was donated the following items:
1.Slide of Thomas F. Burton
2.All military and pension papers
These museums will have Thomas on display, some permanantly such as Fort Pillow, and others on a rotating basis.

All information gathered from the following publications:
"Tennesseans in the Civil War" Volume 1.
"Tennesseans in the Civil War" Volume 2.
"Union Army of Tennessee Adjutants Report"
"Official Records of the Civil War"
"An Untutored Genius: The Military Career of Nathan Bedford Forrest" by Lonnie E. Maness, PH.D.
"Andersonville The Last Depot" by William Marvel
"The Story Of Calloway County" Kirby and Dorothy Jennings
"Dennisons Andersonville Diary" James H. Dennison
"Forts Henry and Donelson the key to the Confederate Heartland" Benjamin Franklin Cooling
"That Devil Forrest Life of Nathan Bedford Forrest" John Allen Wyth

1 *72*

1 Burton Thomas F.

Co _A_, Bradford's Batt'n, *13* Tennessee Cavalry.

3ᵈ Duty Sergt. | *Sergeant*

CARD NUMBERS.

1 *8753025*	26
2 *8753126*	27
3 *8753225*	28
4	29
5	30
6	31
7	32
8	33
9	34
10	35
11	36
12	37
13	38
14	39
15	40
16	41
17	42
18	43
19	44
20	45
21	46
22	47
23	48
24	49
25	50

Book Mark : _____

See also _6 Tenn'l Cav._ _____

Bradford's Batt'n (13 Cav.) Tenn.

Capt. Co. A, Bradford's Batt'n, 13 Tennessee Cav.

Appears on

Company Muster Roll

for ____ Aug. 10 to Dec. 3, 186 ___

Present or absent ____

Stoppage, $ ____ 100 for ____

Due Gov't, $ ____ 100 for ____

Valuation of horse, $ ____ 100

Valuation of horse equipments, $ ____ 100

Remarks: ____

Book mark: ____

(448) ____ Copyist.

Bradford's Batt'n (13 Cav.) Tenn.

Capt. Co. A, Bradford's Batt'n, 13 Tenn. Cav.*

Appears on

Company Muster Roll

for ____ 186 ___

Present or absent ____

Stoppage, $ ____ 100 for ____

Due Gov't, $ ____ 100 for ____

Valuation of horse, $ ____ 100

Valuation of horse equipments, $ ____ 100

Remarks: ____

Book mark: ____

*This company was consolidated with other companies of this battalion, and formed Co. A, H Reg't Tennessee Cavalry (subsequently Co. E, 6 Reg't Tennessee Cavalry).

(858) ____ Copyist.

Bradford's Batt'n (13 Cav.) Tenn.

____ Bradford's Batt'n 13 Tenn. Cav.

Age ____ 32 ____ years.

Appears on

Company Muster-in Roll

of the organization named above. Roll dated ____ 186 3.

Muster-in to date ____ Oct., 186 3.

Joined for duty and enrolled:

When ____ Aug. 1, 186 ___.

Where ____ Paducah, Ky.

Period ____ 3 ____ years.

Valuation of horse, $ ____ 100

Valuation of horse equipments, $ ____ 100

Remarks: ____

Book mark: ____

(856) ____ Copyist.

140

MEMORANDUM FROM PRISONER OF WAR RECORDS. No. _____

(This blank to be used only in the arrangement of said records.)

NAME *	RANK.	No. of Reg't.	State.	Arm of Service.	Co.	Records of—	Vol.	Page.	Vol.	Page.
Austin S. S.	Pvt.	13	Tenn							

Captured at _Fort Pillow, Tenn._ _____, 186_, confined at Richmond, Va., _____, 186 .

Admitted to Hospital at _____

where he died _____, 186 , of _____

Paroled at _____, 186 ; reported at Camp Parole, Md., _____, 186 ;

Copied by _____

MEMORANDUM FROM PRISONER OF WAR RECORDS. No. _____

(This blank to be used only in the arrangement of said records.)

NAME	RANK.	No. of Reg't.	State.	Arm of Service.	Co.	Records of—	Vol.	Page.	Vol.	Page.
									2	46

Captured at _____, 186 , confined at Richmond, Va., _____, 186 .

Admitted to Hospital at _____

where he died _____, 186 , of _____

Paroled at _____, 186 ; reported at Camp Parole, Md., _____, 186 ;

Copied by _____

Pension Number _1:__5:_
B. of ___A., Vol ___4__No _93_

WAR DEPARTMENT,
Surgeon General's Office,
RECORD AND PENSION DIVISION,

Washington, D. C., _____ ___, 186__.

[CERTIFICATE FROM RECORDS.]

It appears, from the records filed in this Office, that _____

_____Co_____, _____Reg't_____Vol_____

was admitted to_____Hospital,_____

_____, 186__, from_____for treatment for

_____

It also appears, as reported by __1__ Surgeon _Commissary General of_
Prisoners, that _Lieut. T. G. Barker_, Co _I_,
_13th_ Reg't _Tenn_ Vol _Cav_, died _July 14th_, 186 _4_, at
Andersonville, Ga. of Diarrhea

Remarks:_____

_____

BY ORDER OF THE SURGEON GENERAL:

_____
Brev. Lieut. Col. and Asst. Surgeon, U. S. Army.
(84)

(NOTE. This certificate should not be detached from the accompanying papers.)

Bot No. 33075

cert. No. 127280

Maranda Burton — widow of

Thomas J Burton

143

Printed and for Sale by C. C. Sholes, Claim Agent, Freeport, Illinois.

WIDOW'S DECLARATION FOR PENSION.

STATE OF *Kentucky*
Calloway COUNTY. } ss.

On this the 15th day of *December* A.D. 186*8*, personally appeared before me, *R. E. Beckham* Clerk of the *Calloway County* Court, within and for the County and State above named, and by Law duly authorized to administer oaths for general purposes, *Maranda Burton* who, after being duly sworn according to law, declares and says that she is aged *thirty seven* years, and that she is a resident of *Murray* in the County of *Calloway* and State of *Kentucky* doth on her oath make the following declaration in order to obtain the benefit of the provision made by the Act of Congress approved July 14, 1862: That she is the widow of *Thos F. Burton* who was a *Seargent* in Company *A* commanded by Captain *John F. Gregory* of the *13th* Regiment of *Tennessee* Volunteers, commanded by ~~Colonel~~ Maj. *F. F. Bradford* in the War of 1861, who *died* at *Andersonville* on or about the day of *July* 186*4*, and the cause of his death was *Sickness* which he *contracted* while in the service of the United States and in his line of duty.

That she was married to the said *Thos F. Burton* on the 21st day of *December 1855* at *Murray* County of *Calloway* State of *Kentucky* by one *C. M. Gateley* a Minister of Gospel and that her name before her said marriage was *Maranda Allbritten*

And that she has remained a widow ever since that period, as will more fully appear by reference to the proof hereto annexed. She further states that at his death her said husband left him surviving only the following named child who was then under the age of sixteen years, that said child resides at *Murray Calloway County Ky* and that the name and date of birth of said child are as follows: *John Thomas Burton, born January the 7th 1864* +

and she hereby constitutes and appoints *Wm E Armstrong* of *Paducah* County of *McCracken* and State of *Kentucky* her lawful attorney to prosecute her said claim, and authorizes him to receive the certificate therefor when ready for delivery. She also declares that she has not in any way been engaged in, or aided, or abetted the rebellion in the United States.

My Post Office address is as follows: *Murray* County of *Calloway* State of *Kentucky*

Signature of *Maranda Burton* Applicant.

Also personally came *Wm H. Allbritten* and *F. S. Oliver* residents of *the* County of *Calloway* State of *Kentucky* persons whom I certify to be respectable and entitled to credit, and who, being duly sworn according to law, say that they were present and saw *Maranda Burton* sign her name (~~or make her mark~~) to the foregoing declaration, and they further swear that they have every reason to believe from the appearance of the applicant and their acquaintance with her that she is the identical person she represents herself to be, and that she still remains the widow of the said *Thos F. Burton* soldier above mentioned who *died* leaving no children under sixteen years of age surviving him other than the above mentioned (*John Thomas Burton*) And that they reside as stated, and have no interest, nor concerned in the prosecution of this claim

Signatures of *William H. Allbritten*
F. S. Oliver

Sworn to and subscribed before me, and I certify that I am not interested in this claim, or concerned in its prosecution; and I further certify that I believe the declarant is the person she represents herself to be. *Witness* my hand and seal of office.
R. E. Beckham Clerk of the *Calloway County Court*

Sir:

I have the honor to acknowledge the receipt from your Office of application for Pension No. 171.500, and to return it herewith, with such information as is furnished by the files of this Office.

It appears from the Rolls on file in this Office, that Thomas F. Burton was enrolled on the 18 day of Augt, 1863, at Paducah Ky. in Co. A, 13th Regiment of (Bradfords Batt'n) Tenn. Volunteers, to serve 3 years, or during the war, and mustered into service as a Sergeant on the 5th day of Dec 1863, at Paducah Ky., in Co. A, 13 Regiment of (Bradford Batt'n) Tenn. (Cavalry) Volunteers, to serve 3 years, or during the war. On the Muster Roll of Co. A of that Regiment, for the months of 186, he is reported

Records on file report him "Died at Andersonville, Ga. July 14. 1864."

I am, Sir, very respectfully,
Your obedient servant,

[signature]
Assistant Adjutant General.

The Commissioner of Pensions
Washington, D. C.

(No. 14.)

Department of the Interior.

PENSION OFFICE.

Feb 17th, 1869

Sir:

You are respectfully requested to furnish official evidence of the date and cause of death of _Thomas F Burton_, who was a _Sergeant_ in Co. _A_, _13th_ Regiment of _Tenn_ Volunteers, who is reported to have died at _Andersonville Ga._ on the _____ day of _July_, 1864, of _____

_____

If the soldier died in hospital, state also at what date he was admitted to the same and for what he was treated.

Please attach this Circular to your report, and return the same to this Office.

Respectfully, &c.,

No. _171,500_

Chris C Cox.
Commissioner.

Surgeon Gen'l, U. S. A.
P. H. B.

146

No 171,500
P. H. B.

Admitted April 169.

C 127.280

file

Surgeon General's Office,

Record and Pension Division

Washington *Feb 31st*, 1868

Respectfully returned to the *Com*
nissioner of Pensions

The enclosed certificate from records,
filed in this Office, being the nearest evidence found, is supposed to relate to the
soldier concerning whom inquiry is made.

BY ORDER OF THE SURGEON GENERAL:

J. J. Woodward

Bvt. Lt. Col. and Asst. Surgeon, U. S. A.

(70)

R. of A., Vol............No............

147

This is to certify that on the 24 of December 1855 I did solemnize the Rights of Matrimony between Thos Burton aged 24 Years, born in Virginia and Maranda Allbritton aged 23 years born in Cal. Co. Ky at the house of Thos Allbritton in the presence of E. Henry and R. Allbritton. Given under my hands this Dec 24th 1855.

C M Gately

Stat of Kentucky Calloway County Set—

I R E Beekham clerk of the County court in and for the County aforesaid do certify that the forgoing is a true copy of an original certificate of marriage between Thos Burton and Maranda Allbritton on file in my office In Testimony of which I hereunto set my hand and affix the seal of said court at Murray Ky this 12th day of January AD 1869. R. E. Beekham clk

Galloway Co. Kentucky Decr. 15th 1868
I hereby certify that I W. M. Mason of the
County of Henry State of Tennessee
was called to attend Mrs. Maranda
Burton (wife of Thomas J. Burton deceased) of the County of Galloway an
State of Kentucky on the 8th day of
January 1864 and at that time was
born a son since named John
Thomas and that I have known the
Child since and that he is still living
at present date

        W. M. Mason, M,

I Sworn to and subscribed
before me this 15th of December 1868.
        Saml McKnight JP.

State of Kentucky Galloway County Set=
I, R. E. Beckham clerk of the County court for
the County aforesaid do certify that Saml
McKnight whose genuine signature appears
to the above certificate is and was at the
time of signing the same an acting Justice
of the Peace in and for Galloway County Ky.
& that his acts as such are entitled to
credit, Given under my hand and seal
of said County this the 15th day of December
A.D. 1868,
        R. E. Beckham Clk

CLAIM FOR WIDOW'S PENSION, WITH MINOR CHILDREN. 127280

BRIEF in the case of *Maranda Burton,* , Widow of

Thomas P. Burton,

Sergeant Co. D. Bradfords Batt 13th Tenn. Cavly.

Resident of *Calloway* County, and State of *Kentucky*

Post Office address: *Murray Calloway County Kentucky*

DECLARATION AND IDENTIFICATION IN DUE FORM.

PROOF EXHIBITED.

Service. *(Adjutant General reports — "Enrolled August 18-1863. And, Died at Andersonville Ga. July 14-1864."*

Death.

Marriage. *December 24th 1865 — Record shows marriage of Thomas Burton and Maranda Albritton on above date.*

Names and dates of birth of children.

	born	, 18	, who will be 16 years old	, 18
		, 18		, 18
		, 18		, 18
John Thomas	*Jany 4th*	, 1864	*Jany 6th*	, 1885
		, 18		, 18
		, 18		, 18
		, 18		, 18
		, 18		, 18
		, 18		, 18

Proof of ages. *Testimony of attending physician at birth*

Loyalty. *Declared.*

Agent, and his P. O. address. *Wm H. Armstrong. Paducah McCracken Co. Ky.*

Issue certificate for *Eight* dollars per month, commencing *July 15th*, 186*7*, and two dollars per month additional for each of the above-named children, commencing *~~~ ~~~* day of *July* , 186*7*.

P. H. Boskan , Examiner.

Passed *April 1st* , 186*7*

APPROVED:

J C F

No. 127.280

Kentucky

Maranda Burton

WIDOW OF

Thomas T Burton

Rank _____ Sergt _____, Co. A,

Regt. Bradfords Batt~n~ 13 Tenn Cav Vols

_____ Louisville _____ Agency.

Rate per Month, $ 8

Commencing _____ 15 July 1864

Additional sum of $2 per Month for each of
the following children, until arriving at the age of
16 years, commencing _____ 25 July 1866

John T _____ 6 Jany 1881

Certificate dated 9 April 1869

Sent to W~m~ H Armstrong
_____ Paducah _____ Ky

Act 14th July, 1862.

Book C Vol. 6 Page 15

_____ Davis _____ Clerk

Burton David. M.

Co _A_, Bradford's Batt'n,
_13_ Tennessee Cavalry.

Corporal	Corporal

CARD NUMBERS.

1	87 53030	26	
2	87 53131	27	
3	8 753228	28	
4		29	
5		30	
6		31	
7		32	
8		33	
9		34	
10		35	
11		36	
12		37	
13		38	
14		39	
15		40	
16		41	
17		42	
18		43	
19		44	
20		45	
21		46	
22		47	
23		48	
24		49	
25		50	

Book Mark :

See also C Tenn Cav

B | Bradford's Batt'n (13 Cav.) | Tenn.

David M. Beerston

Crp., Co. A, Bradford's Batt'n, 13 Tenn. Cav.

Appears on

Company Muster Roll

for Jan'y and Feby, 1864.

Present or absent _Present._

Stoppage, $ _____ 100 for _____

Due Gov't, $ _____ 100 for _____

Valuation of horse, $ _____ 100

Valuation of horse equipments, $ _____ 100

Remarks: _____

*This company was consolidated with other companies of this battalion, and formed Co. A, 14 Reg't Tennessee Cavalry, (subsequently Co. E, 6 Reg't Tennessee Cavalry).

Book mark:

(308)

B | Bradford's Batt'n (13 Cav.) | Tenn.

David M. Beerston

Capt., Co. A, Bradford's Batt'n, 13 Tennessee Cav.

Appears on

Company Muster Roll

for _Aug. 10 to Oct. 31, 1863._

Present or absent _Present._

Stoppage, $ _____ 100 for _____

Due Gov't, $ _____ 100 for _____

Valuation of horse, $ _____ 100

Valuation of horse equipments, $ _____ 100

Remarks: _Adaranus Beauty and ..._

Book mark:

(448)

B | Bradford's Batt'n (13 Cav.) | Tenn.

David M. Beerston

Crp., Co. A, Bradford's Batt'n 13 Tenn. Cav.

Age _21_ years.

Appears on

Company Muster-in Roll

of the organization named above. Roll dated

Paducah, Ky., Dec. 5, 1863.

Muster-in to date _Oct. 24, 1863._

Joined for duty and enrolled:

When _Aug. 26, 1863._

Where _Paducah, Ky._

Period _3_ years.

Valuation of horse, $ _____ 100

Valuation of horse equipments, $ _____ 100

Remarks: _____

Book mark:

(356)

MEMORANDUM FROM PRISONER OF WAR RECORDS. No. _____

(This blank to be used only in the arrangement of said records.)

NAME.	RANK.	ORGANIZATION.				INFORMATION OBTAINED FROM—			
		No. of Reg't	State.	Arm of Service.	Co.	Records of—	Vol.	Page.	Vol.	Page.
Burton, Wm. G	13	Mo.		A		Ohio	2	84		
							4	32		

Captured at _____ , 186 , confined at Richmond, Va., _____ 186 .

Admitted to Hospital at Andersonville Ga

where he died Oct. 11/ _____ , 186 , of _____ ;

Paroled at _____ , 186 ; reported at Camp _____, Md, _____ 186 .

See Burton Wm. _____

Copied by A. H.

ARMY OF THE UNITED STATES.

CERTIFICATE

OF DISABILITY   FOR DISCHARGE.

Sergeant William Allbriten of Captain _____
Company, ("A") of the _13 Tennessee_ Regiment of United States
Cavalry was enlisted by _Lieut. J F Gregory_ of
the _____ Regiment of _____ at _Paducah Ky._
on the _18_ day of _August_ 1863, to serve _3_ years; he was born
in _Calaway_ in the State of _Kentucky_ is _24_
years of age, _5_ feet _11_ inches high, _Fair_ complexion, _Dark_ eyes,
Dark hair, and by occupation when enlisted a _Farmer_ During the last two
months said soldier has been unfit for duty _60_ days.*

STATION : _____

DATE : _____

_____

Commanding Company.

I CERTIFY, that I have carefully examined the said _William Allbriten_ of
Captain _____ Company, and find him incapable of performing the duties of a soldier
because of † _Amputation of left arm in consequence of_
gun-shot wound received in action at Fort Pillow Tenn
April 12 1864. Wishes his discharge in accordance with
Paragraph 1. 40. No 212 186 War dept.
Disability Total

U S General Hospital
Jefferson Barracks Mo
July 16. 64.

Geo F Randolph.
U S A Surgeon.
In charge

DISCHARGED, this _21_ day of _July_ 1864 at _____
Jefferson Barracks Mo

Geo F Randolph
Surg U S A In charge
Commanding the Reg

The soldier desires to be addressed at
Town _____ County _____ State _____

* See Note 1 on the back of this.   † See Note 2 on the back of this.

[A. G. O.-No. 100 & 101—First.]   (DUPLICATES.)

A 13 Cav. Tenn.

William Albritton

Prvt., Co. C, 13 Reg't Tenn. Cav.

Age 24 years.

Admitted Apr. 14, 1864.

To Overton U.S.A. G. H. Memphis, Tenn.

Injury Compound fracture lower third of right arm

W'd at Ft. Pillow, Apr. 12, 1864.

Date of operation Apr. 15, 1864.

Operation Amputation of right arm upper third — flap operation.

Result Returned to duty June 13, 1864.

Surg'l Operations, 2 Quarter 1864; Sheet No. 2.

Watson

A | 13 Cav | Tenn

William Albritton

Rank, Sergt; Co. A, 13 Reg't Tenn. Cav.

Admitted July 18, 1864,

To U. S. A. General Hospital, Jefferson Barracks, near St. Louis, Mo.

From Str. Prairie State

Diagnosis, Amput. L. Arm middle upper 3d

Missile, Round Ball

W'd at Ft. Pillow, Apr. 12, 1864.

Treatm't,

Ret'd to duty , 18 .

Transf'd to I. C. , 18 .

Transf'd to , 18 .

Furloughed , 18 .

Deserted , 18 .

Disch'd from service July 23, 1864.

Died , 18 .

Re-adm'd from furlo' or des'n , 18 .

Remarks:

Age 25

Mo. Reg. No. 724; Hos. No. 3669; Page

Webster

Copyist.

156

ARMY OF THE UNITED STATES.

CERTIFICATE

OF DISABILITY FOR DISCHARGE.

See outside

Carroll Sweeny Private of Captain Lieut Smith's Company, (E) of the Sixth Tennessee Regiment of United States Vols Cavalry was enlisted by Lieut John H Gregory of the Thirteenth Regiment of Tennessee Cavalry at Paducah Kentucky on the Second day of August 1863, to serve Three years; he was born in Wilson County in the State of Tennessee is Thirty Two years of age, Five feet Seven ½ inches high, Dark complexion, Grey eyes, Dark hair, and by occupation when enlisted a Farmer During the last two months said soldier has been unfit for duty 60 days.* He was captured at Fort Pillow Tenn was confined at Andersonville Ga and Florence S.C. where the disease was contracted and constitution destroyed from all appearances as he has not been able for duty since he reported to his Co.

STATION: Pulaski Tennessee

DATE: June 22nd 1865

F. A. Smith
1st Lieut, Co. E 6th Tenn Cav
Commanding Company. E 6 Tenn Cav.

I CERTIFY, that I have carefully examined the said Carroll Sweeny a Private of Captain Lieut Smith's Company, and find him incapable of performing the duties of a soldier because of† Chronic Bronchitis said disease was contracted about Eight Months ago while lying in southern prisons he is unfit for either field service or V. R. C. should urgently recommend his discharge.

Degree of disability one half.

D. C. Tanner
Asst Surgeon.

DISCHARGED, this Fifth day of July 1865, at Pulaski Tenn

W. J. Smith
Col 6th Tenn Cav
Commanding the Reg't.

The soldier desires to be addressed at
Town Smithland County Livingston State Kentucky

* See Note 1 on the back of this. † See Note 2 on the back of this.

[A. G. O. No. 100 & 161—First.] (DUPLICATES.)

8	13 Cav	Tenn	

John C. Simmons

Rank, Pri.; Co. A., 13. Reg't Tenn. Cav.

Admitted .... April 14..., 1864,

To   Overton U. S. A. Gen'l Hosp.
Memphis, Tenn.

From _field_

Diagnosis, Gunshot flesh wound of left
Scapular region ....

.... Missile, _minie Bullet_

W'd at _Ft Pillow April 12_ ...., 1864

Treatm't, _Simple dressings_

Ret'd to duty .... _June 13_ ...., 1864.

Transf'd to I. C. ...., 18 .

Transf'd to ...., 18 .

Furloughed ...., 18 .

Deserted ...., 18 .

Disch'd from service ...., 18 .

Died ...., 18 .

Re-adm'd from furlo' or des'n ...., 18 .

Remarks: ....

age 26

Tenn. Reg. No. 588; Hos. No. 2475; Page ....

            Smart.
(203)   (o 3—074)   Copyist.

S.	13	Cav	Tenn

John C. Simmons

Rank, Prt.; Co. A., 13 Reg't Tenn. Cav.

Admitted .... July 18 ...., 1864,

To   U. S. A. General Hospital,
Jefferson Barracks,
near St. Louis, Mo.

From _Str. Prairie State_

Diagnosis, G. Sh. Wd. left scapula

....

....

.... Missile, ...

W'd at _Fort Pillow_, Ap C 12, 1864.

Treatm't, ...

Ret'd to duty ...., 18 .

Transf'd to I. C. ...., 18 .

Transf'd to ...., 18 .

Furloughed ...., 18 .

Deserted ...., 18 .

Disch'd from service _Oct 22_ ...., 1864.

Died ...., 18 .

Re-adm'd from furlo' or des'n ...., 18 .

Remarks: ....

Mo. Reg. No. 234; Hos. No. 3745; Page ....

            Webster
(203)   (o 3—074)   Copyist.

CASUALTY SHEET.

...

Name: *Elbert Abbert Jones*

Rank: *Bvt. Sergeant*   Company: *B*   Regiment: *13*

Arm: _____   State: *Tennessee*

Nature of Casualty: *Death*

CAUSE OF CASUALTY—(Name of Disease, &c.)	BY WHOM DISCHARGED.

FROM WHAT SOURCE THIS INFORMATION WAS OBTAINED.

Roll furnished by Com'y Gen'l of Prisoners.

DEGREE OF DISABILITY.

BY WHOM CERTIFIED.

Bvt. Major W. S. Hartz, Act'g

REMARKS.

DATE OF DISCHARGE, DEATH, &c.

Sept 1 1864

PLACE OF DISCHARGE, DEATH, &c.

Andersonville Ga.

A. Kenny Clerk.

J. M. Kirkley

(170)

29 | Bradford's Batt'n (13 Cav.) | **Tenn.**

William R. Albritton

Corpl., Co. *A*, Bradford's Batt'n 13 Tenn. Cav.

Age *24* years.

Appears on

Company Muster-in Roll

of the organization named above. Roll dated

Paducah, Ky., *Dec. 5*, 186*3*.

Muster-in to date *Nov. 18*, 186*3*.

Joined for duty and enrolled:

When *Aug. 18*, 186*3*.

Where *Paducah, Ky*

Period *3* years.

Valuation of horse, $ *100*

Valuation of horse equipments, $ *100*

Remarks: ....

....

....

....

....

Book mark: *See Mfr. 64 1871.*

(256) .... *Copyist.*

A | 13 Cav Tenn

William R. Albritton

Co. *A*, *13* Reg't Tenn. Cav.

NOTATION.

Book mark: *Mfn. 64. 1867.*

War Department,

Adjutant General's Office,

Washington, *April 25*, 187*1*.

This man was discharged on Surg's Cert. of Disability July 21. 1864 at Jefferson Bks Mo. This notation supersedes all previous notations made in his case

....

....

....

....

....

....

....

(488) .... *W.B.Allen* *Copyist.*

Printed in the USA
CPSIA information can be obtained
at www.ICGtesting.com
JSHW082211140824
68134JS00014B/551

9 781563 115103